LEARNING A FOREIGN LANGUAGE

LEARNING A FOREIGN LANGUAGE

Understanding the Fundamentals of Linguistics

Alex Poole

ROWMAN & LITTLEFIELD
Lanham • Boulder • New York • London

Published by Rowman & Littlefield
An imprint of The Rowman & Littlefield Publishing Group, Inc.
4501 Forbes Boulevard, Suite 200, Lanham, Maryland 20706
www.rowman.com

6 Tinworth Street, London SE11 5AL, United Kingdom

British Library Cataloguing in Publication Information Available

Library of Congress Cataloging-in-Publication Data

Names: Poole, Alex, author.
Title: Learning a foreign language : understanding the fundamentals of linguistics / Alex Poole.
Description: Lanham, MD : Rowman & Littlefield Publishers, 2020. | Includes bibliographical refer-
ences. | Summary: "This book introduces aspiring bilinguals to second language acquisition
research, but in a way that is accessible to non-specialists and relevant to their lives as language
learners" —Provided by publisher.
Identifiers: LCCN 2020009588 (print) | LCCN 2020009589 (ebook) | ISBN 9781475854176 (cloth) |
ISBN 9781475854190 (epub)
Subjects: LCSH: Second language acquisition.
Classification: LCC P118.2 .P657 2020 (print) | LCC P118.2 (ebook) | DDC 418.0071—dc23
LC record available at https://lccn.loc.gov/2020009588
LC ebook record available at https://lccn.loc.gov/2020009589

CONTENTS

Preface   vii

Introduction   ix

1 Getting and Staying Motivated   1

2 Dealing with Reality: Age, Aptitude, and Smarts   17

3 Comprehension and Enjoyment: The Keys to Acquiring
       Grammar and Vocabulary   33

4 Errors: Keys to Getting Ahead   49

5 The Importance of Being Strategic   65

6 Cultural Awareness: Feelings, Words, and Bodies   81

7 Assess Yourself   101

8 Relax: It's Only a Language   117

About the Author   133

PREFACE

In a sense, this book started the moment I realized the world contained more than one language. That happened when I was a small boy, many years ago. My grandmother's first language was Yiddish, the language of Eastern European Jewry. Both she and my grandfather also spoke French. When I heard these and other languages during childhood, I sensed a certain magic was being performed—and I wanted to be part of the show. It should therefore come as no surprise that my childhood friends had recent roots in Europe and Asia. I loved asking their parents and grandparents about their first languages—Arabic, Frisian, German, Sindhi, and Urdu—and where they learned English.

That Sioux City, Iowa, was the setting might seem unusual, but it really shouldn't. Immigrants have settled all parts of the United States, and multilingual environments aren't limited to major metropolitan areas. In fact, the majority of the world speaks more than one language. For most, it isn't a big deal. Parents sometimes come from different ethnic groups, nations often have multiple cultures, and the languages of school, government, and television are frequently not the ones spoken at home.

While I learned about the normality of language learning from these childhood conversations and extensive travel, it wasn't until graduate school that I understood how it was done. Before that time, I struggled to learn languages. Great initial enthusiasm for Russian, Slovene, and Hebrew quickly waned. Not only were opportunities for practicing these languages quite limited, but American culture placed a low value on attempting to speak them. Discouraging messages about American language learners often involved mockery and emphasized the futility of even trying. That they came from both monolingual Americans and multilingual Europeans didn't help matters.

More significant was my ignorance about the process of language learning. As a late teen and young adult, I had no idea what to do or expect. This was worsened by erroneous beliefs which led to counterproductive practices and unrealistic goals. A PhD in linguistics and years of study helped change all of this, however, and I have achieved my goal of learning another language. While I don't sound like Antonio Banderas and probably never will, I function at a high level in Spanish. Interactions with my Colombian in-laws are no problem, I can understand most written and oral versions of the language, and impromptu conversations get off the ground quite easily. I have even given a few lectures in Spanish.

Most Americans wishing to learn another language won't pursue a doctorate in linguistics. Thankfully, this isn't necessary. Of course, hard work and patience are required, but nature has provided humans with the underlying tools to learn another language. It isn't like being a great athlete or mathematical genius. It is the rule rather than the exception. Learners merely need to understand some fundamentals of the phenomena involved in the process and act accordingly. This book aims to help them do both.

INTRODUCTION

AUDIENCES FOR THIS TEXT

This text is intended for those wishing to learn another language: specifically, individuals who primarily or exclusively speak English. Some readers may have already studied one or several languages, feel frustrated by their lack of progress, and want to move ahead. Others may just be starting their first foreign language and are looking for guidance. Still others may be seriously considering language study but need to find out a little more before making a commitment.

Professional linguists and those with graduate degrees or advanced training in language-related fields should not view the text as breaking new ground, nor should they expect a comprehensive analysis of all issues presented. The dynamics involved in learning multiple languages will not receive coverage in this text. Instead, it will focus on first-time learners. Other than good reading skills, no particular academic background is needed to understand the concepts presented here, making it appropriate for high school students, college language majors, and those independently pursuing a language. Future teachers of any foreign language will find the text relevant for both their students and themselves.

WHAT READERS SHOULD EXPECT

The book's contents can benefit current or would-be language learners who lack the time, background, or desire to consult linguistics texts to gain insight into the process and make informed decisions. Nonspecialists rightfully complain that scholarly books and journals feel impenetrable and fail to generate enthusiasm for learning. While this text captures the knowledge found in academic publications, it packages it in a way that seeks to be both accessible and inspiring.

Each chapter highlights key issues involved in language learning. Readers will receive a general overview of their importance, examine the relevant research, and become aware of the benefits of and obstacles to real-life applications. By doing so, readers will also increase their understanding of the methods and techniques used to generate research questions and analyze data, in addition to fundamental areas of linguistics, such as first-language acquisition, the connection between language and thought, the evolution of language, and culture's relationship to language.

Readers should emerge as informed language learners with a suite of potential ideas for helping themselves and others. However, they will not walk away with one-size-fits-all procedures which guarantee specific outcomes. This is not a how-to book in the typical sense of the term. The challenges of language learning will not magically disappear, nor will readers be prepared to master all aspects of a language within six months. Specific outcomes can't be promised.

HOW TO USE IT

The text can be used as the primary focus of a foreign language pedagogy course, a supplementary text in language classes, a resource for language clubs, or a tool for independent learning. Its chronological arrangement should be followed, as later chapters build on earlier ones. Quickly reading them isn't advised. Occasionally stopping and reflecting will lead to a richer experience. The questions at the end of each chapter review and reinforce relevant concepts and are suitable for both group and individual use. Recommended readings provide more depth or address related topics not covered in chapters.

TERMINOLOGY

Terms are defined within chapters, yet some appear through the entire text. Unless otherwise noted, *language learning* signifies the study of a language other than one's native tongue during the teen and adult years. *Foreign-language learning* sometimes appears to distinguish adolescents and adults from children developing their first language. References may use the phrase *second language*, which involves learning a language in a country where the majority speaks it as their native tongue (e.g., French in France). While interesting, distinctions between *second-* and *foreign-language learning* aren't meaningful in this text.

I

GETTING AND STAYING MOTIVATED

"Why am I getting mad?" "Why am I yelling?" These questions inevitably follow a freak-out because keys can't be instantaneously located. Panic and self-berating also accompany this triviality, yet an almost-Spock-like mind presents itself at health crises, children's academic challenges, and other, far more important events. Maybe it's just copying dad or a genetic predisposition to irrationality. Perhaps bottled-up stress releases itself when nothing is at stake or a suppressed childhood trauma revolves around keys.

Satisfying answers are elusive, but regardless of their significance, most of life's mysteries contain multitudes of complexity. Wise heads should remember journalist H. L. Mencken's assertion that "for every complex problem, there is an answer that is clear, simple, and wrong" (Perry, 2016, para. 11). Psychologist Robert Gardner similarly warns against neatly packaged accounts of language learning motivation, stressing the construct "definitely cannot be assessed by merely asking individuals to give reasons for why they think learning a language is important to them" (Gardner, 2007, p. 10).

Even though self-reports fail to capture the totality of one's motivation, they can highlight key variables that drive language learning. This chapter will discuss how these variables can guide the language learning journey. Specifically, it will explain and exemplify two types of motivation: *extrinsic motivation* and *intrinsic motivation*. There are other ways of conceptualizing motivation (see the end of the chapter for recommended reading), but these two provide an accessible introduction to motivation within language learning research. Readers should think about how their experiences compare to the research presented in the chapter. As motivation is a dynamic phenomenon, readers should consider whether their initial purpose for language learning has changed. Even if it hasn't, they needn't become fearful when it does; as proficiency grows and encounters with the target language multiply, dissimilar motivational impulses and levels of intensity may emerge. In fact, motivation can wildly vacillate in a matter of minutes within individuals, depending on the context (Waninge, de Bot, & Dörnyei, 2014).

TYPES OF MOTIVATION: EXTRINSIC VS. INTRINSIC

Extrinsic Motivation

In most goal-oriented contexts, extrinsic motivation is present to some degree. In terms of general activity, it can be characterized as "doing something because it leads to a separable outcome" (Ryan & Deci, 2000, p. 55). Jogging, for example, often sours the mood of many middle-aged adults, yet they persist because it helps lower blood pressure, control cholesterol, and prevent weight gain. Those same people don't eat skinless chicken breasts and sweet potatoes each night out of spite for hamburgers and French fries; they merely want to avoid open-heart surgery.

Parents sometimes work extra hours not because of an overwhelming interest in their profession but rather to bulk up their kids' college accounts. Children never look forward to garbage night, but they fulfill their obligations to maintain computer privileges, phone time, and access to video games. Millions of Americans obtain jobs merely to put a roof over their head and food on the table.

In 2014–2015, over ten million K–12 students were enrolled in a language class, the majority being Spanish (American Councils for International Education, 2017). Their extrinsic motivation probably revolved around satisfying graduation requirements, getting into college, and obtaining a good job (Pratt, Agnello, & Santos, 2009; Stewart-Strobelt & Chen, 2003). The following two individuals exemplify the value of extrinsic motivation, even if it didn't initially drive their own language learning.

Eric Sargent, an executive at BMW of North America, majored in German and mechanical engineering, yet "did not anticipate the importance of language study to his career and was not overly excited by the language courses available to him" (Fanton, 2017, p. 21). However, his fluency in German has played a critical role in his advancement at the German car company.

Another executive, Trevor Gunn of Medtronic, a medical technology company, can function in Swedish, Russian, and French and credits his success to this fact. Specifically, it has allowed him to be "a significantly better negotiator and business partner, and contributed immensely to my professional growth and chosen path. Command of a foreign language puts you in charge of your future" (Fanton, 2017, p. 2).

Finally, a desire to avoid problems when trying to obtain basic goods and services can also function as an external stimulus to learn a language. For example: An Argentine-born immigrant to Spain in the 1980s would have felt comfortable in Spanish-dominated Barcelona. At the time, Catalan, the regional language, was repressed and excluded from public domains. However, decades of liberalization have made it the city's principal tongue. Instead of diving into Catalan to access its literature, film, and history, the same immigrant today would learn the language to avoid trouble at governmental offices, medical facilities, and other public places.

Intrinsic Motivation

Extrinsic motivation contrasts with *intrinsic motivation*, or "the doing of an activity for its inherent satisfactions rather than for some separable consequence" (Ryan & Deci, 2000, p. 56). Cooking leads to the nourishment of friends and family, but the process itself can be fascinating: kneading dough, chopping vegetables, and melting butter generate satisfying sounds and sensations. Playing tennis produces states of quasiexaltation for amateurs. Slicing backhands, serving, and watching the ball fly are all just plain cool! They represent nothing outside of themselves yet yield enormous fulfillment.

The same can be said of the hordes of people who collect vinyl records. Hours and thousands of dollars can enthusiastically be spent on rare Miles Davis recordings and esoteric Soviet electronica from the 1970s. The newest manifestation of intrinsic motivation in popular culture seems to meld comic books with video games and science fiction celebrities. Fans will spend what seems like a fortune to attend conventions to mingle with like-mined individuals, check out the latest in anime, and stand in line for the autographs and pictures of screen actors and video game designers.

A passion for language learning can manifest itself in many ways, one of which includes amassing language learning materials: textbooks, dictionaries, and literature in a variety of languages. Conjugating verbs in the target language, discovering its vocabulary, and maintaining lists of its notable features occupy endless amounts of time. Etymological discussions, orthographical analyses, and even board games like Scrabble are a few of the pastimes engaged in by those who study language for its own sake.

The late Dr. Donald Steinmetz, a professor of German at Augsburg University in Minneapolis, felt exhilaration when studying languages. One obituary highlighted his "insatiable curiosity, enthusiasm and love of languages" (Harlow, 2010, para. 3) and reported that he "was known to be fluent in at least a dozen languages, and on the rare occasion that a student spoke a language he didn't know, he made an appointment with them and learned it" (para. 2).

Unfortunately, many parents and teachers don't give intrinsic motivation much weight. They believe professional and financial benefits foster optimal motivation; external carrots and sticks can weaken interest in a task, however, and intrinsic motivation has been shown to produce more long-term engagement in and ownership of a task (Deci, Koestner, & Ryan, 2001). Moreover, some language learning research has even suggested the primacy of intrinsic motivation.

One study investigated the motivational levels of English-speaking Canadian adults enrolled in a summer French program. The participants received a questionnaire that inquired about the existence of various categories of motivation in their lives, their perceptions of themselves as learners, and their views of the teacher. The results showed a positive and significant relationship between intrinsic motivation and self-perceived competence. Participants with high intrinsic motivation were less likely to view the teacher negatively and associate the experience with anxiety than those who were mainly extrinsically motivated or reported amotivation (Noels, Clément, & Pelletier, 1999).

Using a similar research tool, the same authors examined the motivational levels of French-speaking Canadian adults enrolled in a summer English program. Unique among the types of motivation considered, intrinsic motivation positively and significantly correlated with all five variables examined: perceived autonomy, perceived competence, motivational intensity, persistence in the study of English, and final grades. Such results, in conjunction with previous studies, led the authors to take a dim view of carrot and stick approaches to motivating language learners: "as long as the reward or punishment is in sight, the subject may engage in learning; once it is removed, however, engagement will likely cease" (Noels, Clément, & Pelletier, 2001, p. 433).

Extrinsic motivation doesn't always trail its intrinsic sibling. One variant of the former known as *identified regulation* appears to foster robust engagement with the language and seems related to intrinsic motivation. It occurs when "individuals invest energy in an activity because they have chosen to do so for personally relevant reasons. In this situation, students would carry out the activity because of its importance for achieving a valued goal" (Noels, Pelletier, Clément, & Vallerand, 2000, p. 62).

For example: Diplomats may study local languages not out of interest or obligation but because they recognize doing so helps them understand the cultures in which they are working. Scholars of ancient warfare may plunge into the study of Latin to gain access to Julius Caesar's writings on the Gallic Wars. Tennis star Rafael Nadal doesn't seem to love English for itself, but he recognizes that international matches and media take place in it.

Kimberly Noels investigated the motivational dispositions of American college students in first- and second-semester Spanish classes and found a positive and significant correlation between this type of motivation and its intrinsic counterpart. In fact, identified regulation was the strongest type of motivation reported by participants (Noels, 2001). A similar study examined Canadian college students' motivational dispositions toward Japanese and discovered that identified regulation and intrinsic motivation were the two most influential types of motivation, respectively (McEwon, Noels, & Saumure, 2014).

Two other studies investigated a mix of monolingual Canadian college students and heritage language learners (i.e., the children of one or more parents who speak the target language natively). In the first, heritage learners reported that identified regulation was the most important reason to study German, followed by intrinsic motivation, while the reverse was true for monolinguals (Noels, 2005). In the second study, identified regulation was the most important reason to study Chinese for both groups, while intrinsic motivation was second for monolinguals yet fell to third for heritage language learners (Comanaru & Noels, 2009).

WHICH ONE IS BETTER?

Readers may feel confused. Extrinsic motivation may have seemed good, but intrinsic motivation seemed better. However, the last couple of paragraphs appear to call that assessment into question. So, which one, in fact, is better: intrinsic or extrinsic motivation? There is no clear answer. Differing circumstances probably determine the influence of each type. An international student wanting to pursue a doctorate at an American university may have zero interest in the English language but will be strongly motivated to learn English. Rejection from graduate programs would obviously eliminate such motivation.

On the other hand, a native speaker of English might study Italian during college due to intrinsic motivation. While love of Italian literature and linguistics may have initiated and sustains her engagement with the language, its intensity could diminish due to work requirements and family obligations.

In reality, most long-term American adult language learners probably possess varying degrees of both intrinsic and extrinsic motivation. The following college student's shame demonstrates *introjected regulation* (i.e., a type of extrinsic motivation focused on escaping feelings of guilt or raising one's self-esteem): "It's embarrassing to be Chinese physically and find yourself in a situation where you can no longer speak the language (especially since you were once very fluent in it) to other Chinese people" (Comanaru & Noels, 2009, p. 149).

That same student also reported feeling intrinsically motivated to learn Chinese: "It is fascinating to finally have characters and words to these sounds that I know. It's strange to only know a language orally, but I definitely love learning how to read and write" (Comanaru & Noels, 2009, p. 149).

One type of motivation may also lead to another. Many Americans, for example, have spouses from other countries. In order to communicate with their in-laws and understand their culture, these individuals study the language spoken by the bride- or groom-to-be. After obtaining a proficiency level that allows for meaningful interaction with native speakers and basic cultural understanding, extrinsic motivation often wanes. However, while working toward their goals, a love of the structures, sounds, and use of the language may develop.

THE MIXED MOTIVATIONS OF FAMOUS LANGUAGE LEARNERS

The lives of famous (and successful) language learners exemplify the complexity of motivation. Like many young males who seek adventure abroad, novelist Joseph Conrad undoubtedly pictured himself in exotic circumstances, speaking languages other than his native Polish. The famed author of *Heart of Darkness*, an English-language novel about European colonialism in Africa, Conrad initially learned languages out of necessity. Early in life, he added Russian due to Czarist control of his birthplace, German because of his contact with the large German ethnic population that surrounded him, and Latin from school (Pousada, 1994).

His exposure to French was social and literary. A French governess cared for him as a child, and his father translated French drama into Polish. Although romantic accounts of his seemingly miraculous absorption of English while working as a seaman make for good theater, he already had experienced some contact with English (his father translated Shakespeare into Polish), but he struggled to pass navigational tests, due in part to insufficient English proficiency (Pousada, 1994).

In short, Conrad was motivated by extrinsic forces. But it is clear that he also loved, or at least was obsessed with, the language in which he produced his largest body of work, English. In particular, he enjoyed the "'plastic' freedoms of his adopted tongue" (Lichtig, 2015, para. 5), and felt English was "more tolerant and flexible" (Pousada, 1994, p. 340). He wrote the novel *Lord Jim* in English but incorporated French, Spanish, and Italian into it, which Sylvère Monod calls "polyglot wordplay" (Monod, 2005, p. 222).

Another figure who illustrates mixed motivations is the late polyglot journalist, essayist, and novelist Arthur Koestler. Intense, exotic, and well traveled would best describe his life and work. He is probably most known for his novel *Darkness at Noon*, an attack on Soviet leader Joseph Stalin's crimes against humanity and the false promises of communism. Jailed for being a communist spy during the Spanish Civil War, Koestler was witness to most twentieth-century political movements, including Zionism, which led him to Israel for a time and some proficiency in Hebrew (Avishai, 1990).

Koestler was apparently able to function in German and French at three years of age (Avishai, 1990). He also knew the Hungarian of the city in which he was raised—Budapest—and likely had some passive knowledge of Yiddish due to his Jewish background. He could also speak Russian and Spanish (Menand, 2009). His motivation to learn Spanish appears to be mostly extrinsic. As a journalist, he needed it to cover the events of the Spanish Civil War. His subsequent study of it to prevent madness while imprisoned in the city of Málaga is a nightmarish example of language-learning motivation (Scammell, 2001).

Earlier in life, Koestler had found meaning in Zionism and thus moved to British Palestine and set about learning Hebrew. Although his study of the language seemed to be based on integrating into the local Jewish community and rebuilding the Jewish homeland, his decision to abandon it was caused, in part, by his intrinsic dislike of the language and particular disdain for the "'obsolete and cumbersome' Hebrew alphabet, which made reading the language difficult" (Safran, 2005, p. 49).

Unlike Koestler, Irish playwright Samuel Beckett wasn't raised in a multilingual environment. Born at the beginning of the twentieth century in Dublin, he had no immediate need to write in French. He didn't flee his country of birth, nor was the literary landscape of his native language—English—without suitable venues for publication. Quite simply, he loved the French language, but he also used it to achieve a minimalist mode of expression which his native language would not allow him (Dewaele, 2007). He even went so far as to say, "In French it is easier to write without style" (Power, 2016, para. 7).

PRACTICAL ADVICE

Few twenty-first-century Americans will lead lives like Beckett, Koestler, and Conrad, and thus more practical ways of maintaining motivation are needed. Initial motivations may have arrived with minimal effort. Inspiration to learn could have been falling in love or a job opportunity that required proficiency in another language. But motivation is not always on autopilot. It ebbs and flows. Just like a relationship, it requires work and intentionality. In short, learners will explicitly have to ask themselves "How can I motivate myself to keep going?"

Ignoring this reality can lead to complacency once certain goals are met. The learner who never imagined herself being able to function in Swahili, for example, can now comfortably understand newspapers in that language and carry on conversations at the campus dining hall with international students from Tanzania. The dream has been fulfilled, so the tension that propelled her daily study has vanished. Such a student is at risk of plateauing.

An active imagination facilitates motivation. The student desiring admission into a graduate program in Germany may envision herself speaking the language at international conferences and having peers, friends, and relatives marvel at her proficiency. The young professional studying Italian might imagine herself taking afternoon strolls with her Roman boyfriend, eating gelato, and sipping fine wine. Educational linguist Zoltan Dörnyei explains that such visions "reduce the discrepancy between our actual and ideal selves" (Dörnyei, 2008, p. 3) and thus constitute strong motivational tools.

Interestingly, associating romantic fantasies with language learning is quite common. The language-learning app Babbel surveyed three thousand native speakers of English and found that most Americans (71 percent) viewed bilingualism as sexy, and 53 percent of men fantasized about foreign women (Howard, 2016). International love is not, however, the exclusive domain of Western males. In Japan, some women blend learning English with the wish to date an attractive Hollywood star like Brad Pitt or Tom Cruise. In response, language schools have been known to include photos of white, male teachers in advertising (Piller & Takahashi, 2006).

A motivational repertoire could also include learners imagining using the target language in their future career. This type of extrinsic motivation, referred to above as *identified regulation* (Noels, Pelletier, Clément, & Vallerand, 2000), would be best suited for those whose jobs contain an international component. Undergraduate students wishing to pursue graduate studies in virtually any humanities or arts field may not see the relevance of learning a classical or modern language, but they should utilize this type of motivation if they want to possess reading abilities in two languages—a typical requirement for graduation.

Obtaining the accolades held by admired individuals, a type of extrinsic motivation known as *external regulation* (Dörnyei, 1994) is another option. Wanting to be like Joseph Conrad, Arthur Koestler, or Samuel Beckett could spur those in the literary world, yet models need not be as grandiose. Learning the language of a religious tradition (e.g., Hebrew, Arabic, Sanskrit), a heritage language spoken by immigrant grandparents, or something seemingly exotic and difficult (e.g., Chinese, Japanese) will likely win praise from family, friends, and the local community.

Introjected regulation (Dörnyei, 1994) may be a long-term burden on the soul, but it can provide short-term engagement for all learners when used in moderation, not just heritage learners embarrassed about poor proficiency in their parents' language (Comanaru & Noels, 2009). A student pursuing a degree in international business may have already taken the two years of college French required by their degree program, yet they know they can barely carry on a conversation and feel there is something shameful and almost fraudulent about claiming possession of credentials to work in a non-English-speaking environment.

Physical manifestations of motivation need not be complex. Actions as simple as spontaneously addressing native speakers can release a shot of dopamine. When a couple debates the value of a supermarket product, learners can chime in with their opinion. If a crying child is present, words of consolation can be offered or jokes about the challenges of parenthood can be made. At restaurants and bakeries, employees can be asked about their background, family, and opinion on political matters—or even soccer!

Of course, strangers should be approached with caution, and opportunities for such interaction may rarely present themselves outside of major metropolitan areas. Other sources of motivation require neither a large population nor much of a time commitment. While washing dishes or ironing clothes for the next day, learners could watch a Spanish-language soap opera or *telenovela*. If one prefers comedy, reruns of the iconic Mexican sitcom *El Chavo* can be found on numerous channels. Serious topics aren't preferable; the goal is to engage the language through something enjoyable.

Likewise, there is nothing wrong with watching Spanish-language versions of American and British movies. Most cable, satellite, and subscription-based streaming providers hold large collections of Hollywood hits dubbed into Spanish or with Spanish-language subtitles, in addition to original documentaries and films produced in Latin America and Spain. For those in large urban areas, Spanish-language movie theaters, as well as live theaters, may be available. Again, language learning will be the by-product of motivation to consume enjoyable media.

If a more exotic language is the target, its television and movie presence probably won't reach the level occupied by Spanish. However, because of the rapid evolution of digital technology, legions of podcasts in multiple languages and on numerous topics are easily downloadable. History and travel programs from Romania, daily news from Egypt, and documentaries about various Japanese cultural issues can fill an MP3 player.

During a miserably hot, ten-minute walk from car to office, the mind can find distraction by focusing on the adjectives and adverbs that pop up in podcasts on topics like the Inquisition and Parkinson's disease. A litany of programs can accompany daily commutes or long-distance drives to visit friends and family. While passengers are conked out, the driver can concentrate on the intonation patterns that emanate from a little electronic device—and on the road, of course.

While relaxing at home, between classes, during work breaks, and on the bus, pleasure reading can respond to intrinsic motivation to engage interesting topics; at the same time, language is being learned—even if the initial motivational intensity for language study, per se, has decreased. As with television shows, movies, and podcasts, these texts need not be medieval treatises which are only understood by scholars. Supermarket books (i.e., those easy-to-read books found in the grocery store checkout aisle), in fact, fulfill both desires. Louis L'Amour's novels about crime, cattle, and love on the Great Plains, for example, were written in English yet are just as entertaining and easy to comprehend in Spanish.

Finally, a natural sense of competitiveness with learners of the same language can be utilized. If kept private, the urge to outshine a peer in class or in the presence of native speakers can prove potent. This impulse involves four parts:

- comparing the individual's grammar, vocabulary, and pronunciation to one's own
- determining which person speaks faster

- counting the number of times both switch to English
- noting native speakers' willingness to engage in the target language with each person.

An activity that also boosts motivation is self-assessment. Later chapters will provide a more in-depth treatment of this topic, but for now, it is important to be aware of the strength of monitoring language growth. Maintaining daily language diaries, comparing writing samples completed months apart, and listening to old audio recordings of oneself and noting differences in grammar, vocabulary, speed, and pronunciation are all simple ways of doing this that don't require expertise in linguistics or social science research methods.

Linguist and archaeologist Elizabeth Barber was doing such things when she noticed the emergence of the "Din in the Head." This fascinating and motivating phenomenon occurs during extensive immersive situations—written or spoken—and refers to the unintentional practice of the target language as a result of being inundated with challenging yet intelligible vocabulary, grammar, and pronunciation. Oftentimes, learners accurately utilize forms they don't consciously understand (Krashen, 1983).

On a trip to the former Soviet Union, Barber had to use Russian with her monolingual guides. After a few days of struggling to find the language, the language found her and eventually rolled off her tongue: "The constant rehearsal of these phrases of course was making it easier and easier to speak quickly and quickly; things popped out as prefabricated chunks" (Krashen, 1983, p. 42).

A FINAL THOUGHT

A final thought has nothing to do with intrinsic or extrinsic motivation but rather is a simple observation: Millions, perhaps billions, of individuals have learned or are learning another language. They work in various industries, study in universities, and carry on relationships in tongues not native to them. Are they somehow geniuses? Do they possess skills inaccessible to readers of this text? The answer to both of these questions is clearly *no*. In short, learning a language is a natural process available to all of humanity.

This necessity of maintaining motivation, however, feels taxing. Why can't Americans be like Europeans, who seem to just know English? How can some learn a language with what seems to be such little effort? Europeans learn English in school and are surrounded by English-language television, movies, and books. Most Americans, on the other hand, are adults or late adolescents when they come to their senses. Age doesn't slam the door on bilingualism, but it changes the way to approach it.

And while there are a few individuals who seem naturally gifted with languages, the popular interpretation of their abilities doesn't match reality. The next chapter will expose myths and present facts about age and language learning. As will be demonstrated, the average bilingual is no genius. Fortunately for most adult language learners, this is good news.

DISCUSSION QUESTIONS

1. Who or what initially inspired you to learn a language?
2. What are some of your extrinsic motivations to learn another language?
3. What are some of your intrinsic motivations to learn another language?
4. Find a bilingual immigrant in your community. Ask them to explain whether extrinsic or intrinsic motivation has been stronger for them.
5. How has this chapter changed your views on motivation?

RECOMMENDED READING

Dörnyei, Z. (2010). Researching motivation: From integrativeness to the ideal L2 self. In S. Hunston & D. Oakley (Eds.), *Introducing applied linguistics: Concepts and skills* (pp. 74–83). London: Routledge.

In this piece, Zoltan Dörnyei summarizes and critiques two other ways of framing motivation: *integrative motivation*—"the desire to learn an L2 of a valued community so that one can communicate with members of the community and sometimes even to become like them" (p. 74)—and *in-*

strumental motivation, which refers to "the concrete benefits that language proficiency might bring about (e.g., career opportunities, increased salary)" (p. 74). Specifically, he shows how decades of research have impacted how these terms are treated in research and practice.

REFERENCES

American Councils for International Education. (2017). *The national K–12 foreign language enrollment survey report.* Retrieved from https://www.americancouncils.org/sites/default/files/FLE-report-June17.pdf.
Avishai, B. (1990). Koestler and the Zionist revolution. *Salmagundi, 87,* 234–259.
Comanaru, R., & Noels, K. (2009). Self-determination, motivation, and the learning of Chinese as a heritage language. *The Canadian Modern Language Review, 66,* 131–158. doi:10.3138/cmlr.66.1.131
Deci, E., Koestner, R., & Ryan, R. (2001). Extrinsic rewards and intrinsic motivation in education: Reconsidered once again. *Review of Educational Research, 71,* 1–27. doi: 10.3102/00346543071001001
Dewaele, J. (2007). Becoming bi- or multi-lingual later in life. In P. Auer & L. Wei (Eds.), *Handbook of multilingualism and multilingual communication* (pp. 89–118). Berlin: De Gruyter.
Dörnyei, Z. (1994). Motivation and motivating in the foreign language classroom. *The Modern Language Journal, 78,* 273–284. doi: 10.1111/j.1540-4781.1994.tb02042.x
Dörnyei, Z. (2008). New ways of motivating foreign language learners: Generating vision. *Links, 38,* 3–4. Retrieved from http://www.zoltandornyei.co.uk/uploads/2008-dornyei-links.pdf
Fanton, J. (2017). *America's languages: Investing in language education for the 21st century.* Cambridge, MA: American Academy of Arts and Sciences. Retrieved from https://www.amacad.org/content/publications/publication.aspx?d=22474
Gardner, R. (2007). Motivation and second language acquisition. *Porta Linguarum, 8,* 9–20. Retrieved from http://www.ugr.es/~portalin/articulos/PL_numero8/1-R%20C%20%20GADNER.pdf
Harlow, T. (2010, January 4). Don Steinmetz was a "genius" of languages. *The Minneapolis Star Tribune.* Retrieved from http://www.startribune.com/don-steinmetz-was-a-genius-of-languages/80671837/
Howard, L. (2016, August 24). Bilinguals are more attractive, say most Americans, and here's why. *Bustle.* Retrieved from https://www.bustle.com/articles/180441-bilinguals-are-more-attractive-say-most-americans-and-heres-why
Krashen, S. (1983). The din in the head, input, and the Language Acquisition Device. *Foreign Language Annals, 16,* 41–44. doi: 10.1111/j.1944-9720.1983.tb01422.x|
Lichtig, T. (2015, December 10). Why writing in English was a good career move for Nabokov, Conrad—and now Chirovici. *The Telegraph.* Retrieved from https://www.telegraph.co.uk/books/what-to-read/why-writing-in-english-was-a-good-career-move-for-nabokov-conrad/
McEwon, M., Noels, K., & Saumure, K. (2014). Students' self-determined and integrative orientations and teachers' motivational support in a Japanese as a foreign language context. *System, 45,* 227–241. doi: 10.1016/j.system.2014.06.001
Menand, L. (2009, December 21). Road warrior: Arthur Koestler and his century. *The New Yorker.* Retrieved from https://www.newyorker.com/magazine/2009/12/21/road-warrior
Monod, S. (2005). Joseph Conrad's polyglot wordplay. *The Modern Language Review, 100,* 222–234.

Noels, K. (2001). Learning Spanish as a second language: Learners' orientations and perceptions of their teachers' communication styles. *Language Learning, 51,* 107–144. doi: 10.1111/ 0023-8333.00149

Noels, K. (2005). Orientations to learning German: Heritage language learning and motivational substrates. *The Canadian Modern Language Review, 62,* 285–312. doi: 10.3138/ cmlr.62.2.285

Noels, K., Clément, R., & Pelletier, L. (1999). Perceptions of teachers' communicative style and students' intrinsic and extrinsic motivation. *The Modern Language Journal, 83,* 23–34. doi: 10.1111/0026-7902.00003

Noels, K., Clément, R., & Pelletier, L. (2001). Intrinsic, extrinsic, and integrative orientations of French-Canadian learners of English. *The Canadian Modern Language Review, 57,* 424–442. doi: 10.3138/cmlr.57.3.424

Noels, K., Pelletier, L., Clément, R., & Vallerand, R. (2000). Why are you learning a second language? Motivational orientations and self-determination theory. *Language Learning, 50,* 57–85. doi: 10.1111/0023-8333.00111

Perry, M. (2016, November 8). On Election Day, some quotes from H. L. Mencken on elections, voting and democracy [Blog post]. Retrieved from http://www.aei.org/publication/on-election-day-some-quotes-from-h-l-mencken-on-elections-voting-and-democracy/

Piller, I., & Takahashi, K. (2006). A passion for English: Desire and the language market. In A. Pavlenko (Ed.), *Bilingual minds: Emotional experience, expression, and representation* (pp. 59–83). Clevedon, UK: Multilingual Matters.

Pousada, A. (1994). Joseph Conrad's multilingualism: A case study of language planning in literature. *Journal of English Studies, 75,* 335–349. doi:10.1080/00138389408598925

Power, C. (2016, July 7). Samuel Beckett, the maestro of failure. *The Guardian.* Retrieved from https://www.theguardian.com/books/booksblog/2016/jul/07/samuel-beckett-the-maestro-of-failure

Pratt, C., Agnello, M., & Santos, S. (2009). Factors that motivate high-school students' decisions to study Spanish. *Hispania, 92,* 800–813.

Ryan, R., & Deci, E. (2000). Intrinsic and extrinsic motivations: Classic definitions and new directions. *Contemporary Educational Psychology, 25,* 54–67. doi:10.1006/ceps.1999.1020

Safran, W. (2005). Language and nation-building in Israel: Hebrew and its rivals. *Nations and Nationalism, 11,* 45–63. doi: 10.1111/j.1354-5078.2005.00191.x

Scammell, M. (2001). Arthur Koestler in Civil War Spain. *AGNI, 54,* 86–104.

Stewart-Strobelt, J., & Chen, H. (2003). Motivations and attitudes affecting high school students' choice of foreign language. *Adolescence, 38,* 161–170.

Waninge, F., de Bot, K., & Dörnyei, Z. (2014). Motivational dynamics in language learning: Change, stability, and context. *The Modern Language Journal, 98,* 704–723. doi: 10.1111/ j.1540-4781.2014.12118.x

2

DEALING WITH REALITY: AGE, APTITUDE, AND SMARTS

It's doubtful most readers grew up in Holland, Sweden, or Denmark. If they had, they'd probably already know at least one other language and consider bilingualism a done deal. International students from these countries speak of their English proficiency like an American speaks of owning a car: it's just something everybody does. Visitors to Amsterdam, for instance, will quickly encounter a world of English speakers: homeless drug addicts, street merchants, and café workers regularly chat about sports, politics, and food in a language different from their native one.

Instruction begins in elementary school and continues into high school. An environment rich in English print reinforces coursework. Up to half of television offerings may be in English, and at least 30 percent of BBC subscribers view shows without subtitles (Edwards, 2014). A relatively recent report on multilingualism in the European Union found that 94 percent of Dutch citizens reported knowing another language, and 77 percent possess "practical skills in at least two foreign languages" (European Commission, 2012, p. 13).

In the same study, 44 percent of Swedes reported having the ability to converse in two languages (European Commission, 2012). A more recent survey ranked Sweden third out of seventy-two countries in which English is not the native language. Its "very high proficiency" classification suggests the average citizen can "use nuanced and appropriate language in social situations; read advanced texts with ease; and negotiate a contract with a native English speaker" (Education First, 2016, p. 9).

Denmark also regularly ranks high in English proficiency. Danish scientists reported that more than 50 percent of their publications involve colleagues from other countries (Education First, 2016). Likewise, 41 percent of Danes utilize a foreign language on a daily basis, while 71 percent and 69 percent, respectively, often consume media and surf the internet in a language other than Danish. Finally, 64 percent view learning a language as necessary for studying abroad (European Commission, 2012).

Surveys show Americans are radically less willing and able to speak another language. One Gallup poll revealed that only 17 percent of white Americans feel learning a language is "essential," while 32 percent consider it "not important" (Jones, 2013). The same poll also showed only 34 percent of Americans could carry on a basic conversation in another language. More recent statistics suggest that number will soon drop: fewer public elementary, middle, and high schools provided foreign language instruction in 2008 than in 1987 (Fanton, 2017).

Of those who do claim to speak another language, 75.5 percent learned it from family members. Unfortunately, there is no surplus of language teachers waiting for potential students. Most states (forty-four) cannot recruit a sufficient number of language teachers; in response, some states, such as Maine, "are cutting programs and pondering lower standards because of the shortage" (Feinberg, 2016, para. 1). In fact, during the 2007–2008 school year, 21 percent of American high schools offered no language classes ("Language Instruction," 2017).

Slightly more than half of American colleges included languages in their general education requirements during the 2009–2010 academic year (Skorton & Altschuler, 2012). College language enrollments decreased from 2009 to 2013, with Spanish (−8.2 percent), French (−8.1 percent), Italian (−11.3 percent), Japanese (−7.8 percent), and Arabic (−7.5 percent) showing notable losses. Only a minority of languages (e.g., Korean, Portuguese, and Chinese) demonstrated numerical additions (Goldberg, Looney, & Lusin, 2015).

The typical language-learning experience for the average college-educated American consists of a few years during high school and a couple of semesters at college. Many students possess a mixture of low enthusiasm and a bit of resentment when faced with language requirements. Teachers and professors fear massive failure rates, constant student complaints, and parental whining if they employ rigorous standards in the classroom. A handful of language nerds go on to actually learn something, but most don't give the subject a second thought after their last final exam.

Even America's intellectual elite is shamefully monolingual. The negativity literary theorist Doug Steward describes surrounding language study during his graduate work in the late 1970s is unlikely to have improved and probably extends beyond humanities departments and into other areas of academia:

> I found little support for foreign language study in printed departmental requirements or rationales and observed that, by and large, graduate students in my department and others typically treated the requirement as a nuisance and lost their "reading knowledge" as soon as the exam was over. (Steward, 2006, p. 204)

WHY DON'T AMERICANS MAKE THE GRADE?

This discouraging state of affairs could reflect a linguistic laziness that comes with speaking the world's dominant language. After all, English is the lingua franca of international business (Neeley, 2012), the most commonly used language on the internet, and represents the language of choice for published scientific research (Jha, 2011). Another possibility is that a critical mass of Americans believe that *they* just aren't good at learning languages and thus put minimal effort into it.

Regrettably, research dating from the mid-1980s up to the present day demonstrates that large percentages of Americans feel their compatriots don't have the capacity to learn another language (Horwitz, 1988; Latomaa, 1998; Le, 2004). One CEO and founder of a network of charter schools in New York City even expressed this sentiment when trying to justify the elimination of language instruction: "Americans don't tend to do foreign languages very well. I think if I were doing schools in Europe I might feel differently. But my son took three years of French and he could barely say, 'How are you?'" (Kohli, 2014, para. 2).

AGE DOES MAKE A DIFFERENCE: THE CRITICAL PERIOD

Happily, there is no evidence that one's nationality plays a role in innate language-learning abilities; however, there is evidence for age playing a role in humans' ability to learn a language. This obviously concerns Americans because, unlike most Europeans, they usually don't pursue language learning with any gusto until adulthood (or very late adolescence)—if they do it at all. And many among them take a binary position on the matter: children can learn languages easily; adults will struggle and not get very far.

Research suggests American adults have held this view for some time. In 1988, University of Texas researcher Elaine K. Horwitz investigated the beliefs of first-semester college language students and found more than 75 percent believed that children learn languages with less effort than adults (Horwitz, 1988). More than a decade later, an investigation of approximately one thousand American undergraduates of various proficiency levels studying more than a dozen languages showed comparable results (Rifkin, 2000).

The First Language

But before addressing how age actually impacts the ability to learn another language, its role in first-language development should be examined. For humans, there likely is a *critical period*, or developmental stage, during which their first language can emerge. In 1967, psychologist Eric Lenneberg posited that children who reach puberty without regular contact with language won't develop it. He speculated that as the brain matures, its ability to host new skills atrophies. In short, by the age at which language normally becomes lateralized to the left hemisphere, the probability of developing it—if not already present—is extremely low (Friedmann & Rusou, 2015).

More recent work has specified possible mechanisms responsible for this phenomenon, such as the equilibrium of excitatory and inhibitory neurotransmitters during early childhood (Friedmann & Rusou, 2015). Exactly when this critical period—or sensitive period, as it is sometimes called—begins and ends has been debated since almost immediately after the appearance of Lenneberg's work. Also unclear are the speed and severity of the loss of language-learning abilities.

Tragically, cases of child abandonment have verified Lenneberg's general position. Genie, a thirteen-year-old girl who had been abused and neglected by her family since birth, was removed from her home in 1970 by child welfare officials in Los Angeles. They quickly discovered she possessed limited verbal skills and employed therapists, linguists, and physicians to help rectify this situation. Sadly, more than half a decade of hard work resulted in little progress (Johnson & Newport, 1989).

About 170 years prior to her birth, an adolescent boy named Victor appeared in the outskirts of Aveyron, France. Although the exact circumstances of his early life remain a mystery, they probably involved limited human contact due to parental desertion. Like Genie, he knew little language and possessed no human socialization skills. Jean-Marc Gaspard Itard, a physician interested in working with deaf children, tried to teach Victor language, but with little success (Simpson, 2007).

Physiological problems can also impede language development. Unnoticed hearing impairments and a thiamin deficiency before a child's first birthday, for example, create circumstances under which appropriate levels of linguistic stimulation are not present, causing concerns about affected individuals' capacity to obtain typical proficiency in their first language (Friedmann & Rusou, 2015).

The Foreign Language

Applied to foreign-language learning, the critical period seems daunting, at least initially. It suggests that native-like use of the target language depends on prepubescent fluency. While no magic birthday milestone turns off the learning switch, later learning seems to present disadvantages. This is what a large-scale study carried out in the early 2000s found. A group of researchers utilized 1990 census data to discover the age at which the critical period ends. Information relating to self-reported English proficiency, current age, age of initial exposure, and educational attainment was collected from more than 2.3 million immigrants (Hakuta, Bialystok, & Wiley, 2003).

The results indicated that education seems to ameliorate some of the negative impacts of age; nevertheless, the results confirmed that "the degree of success in second-language-acquisition steadily declines throughout the life span" (Hakuta, Bialystok, & Wiley, 2003, p. 37), with age of exposure to English playing a significant role in long-term outcomes. Two years later, a review of four decades of research involving multiple target languages showed the negative impact of age on grammar and pronunciation (DeKeyser & Larson-Hall, 2005).

Studies on the brains of bilinguals show differences between those whose initial exposure to another language is relatively early—before the tween years—and those who encounter it later (post-tween years). While the former exhibit the left-hemisphere activity and language specialization typical of native speakers, the latter demonstrate much greater use of both hemispheres, suggesting some degree of reliance on general learning mechanisms for the purposes of foreign-language learning and use (Schouten, 2009).

However, there is not agreement among scientists about the relationship of such structural differences to postadolescents' ability to produce native-like or near native-like speech. Other questions remain about the critical period, such as the influence of gender, the accuracy of measurement tools, the role of intervening variables such as educational level, intensity of exposure to the target language, and the significance of linguistic aptitude (Birdsong & Molis, 2001; Flege, Yeni-Komshian, & Liu, 1999; Scovel, 2000; Mayberry & Kluender, 2018).

Regardless of the theoretical disputes and unanswered questions about the critical period, simple observation shows most adult language learners cannot pass as native speakers of the target language. Even after more than a decade of intensive Spanish study, they may still struggle to roll the word-initial *R* and require intense mental and physical preparation to correctly pronounce words like *Ricardo, río,* and *roto*. The unrolled *R* in *caro* (expensive) is often said when *carro* (car)—rolled *R* required—is really meant.

Multisyllabic words like *debilitamiento* (weakening) and *arroz masacotudo* (crunchy and dry rice) might require a rehearsal or two for publicly intelligible production. Concentration is often still required to say the *S* sound on words that end with *Z* (e.g., luz, González, Gomez) and to remember the two forms of *for* in Spanish: I did it *for* you (Lo hice *para* tí), and I did it *because* of you (Lo hice *por* tí). To make hypothetical statements in English, the simple past tense form of the verb often suffices (e.g., *If I had* a bicycle . . . or *If you wanted* to tell me something). Spanish has separate forms for such things, which are perpetually tricky for English speakers.

English teachers and their students can name a litany of pronunciation and grammar issues that pose eternal challenges for non-native speakers after the critical period. More than a few cannot consistently pronounce the voiced and voiceless *TH* sounds (e.g., there and think) and instead pronounce them with variations of *D* and *S* sounds (e.g., der/ser, dink/sink). In many East Asian languages, clear distinctions between *R* and *L* don't exist. As a result, words like *rice* and *lice* often sound the same, and the name *Luna* can manifest as *Runa*.

Decades of exposure, degrees from English-medium universities, speaking and writing in English for thousands of hours, and relative isolation from their first languages can't shield non-native speakers who started learning English after adolescence from incorrect use of the third-person singular present tense. The verbs in sentences like *He likes to eat ice cream frequently* and *She eats a lot of salad* often omit the suffix *S* and come out as *He like to eat ice cream frequently* and *She eat a lot of salad*.

The article system likewise troubles learners for many years. Three monosyllabic words native speakers rarely think about—*the, an, a*—often find themselves erroneously used in the writing of otherwise brilliant international students. Finally, the English prepositional system (e.g., on, at, to, over, under, below, between) is difficult to understand and hard to learn. Students' questions often flummox teachers: Why do people say both "I want to speak *with* you" and "I want to speak *to* you"? Why do people get *on* a plane yet *in* a car? What is the difference between "Get *off* me" and "Get *off of* me"? Clear and concise answers are often elusive or nonexistent.

Linguists can only speculate as to why humans lose the ability to go native linguistically as they age. One intuitively appealing explanation focuses on the organization of hunter-gatherer societies. Unlike contemporary societies, these early humans lived in small groups and didn't possess modern tools (e.g., identification cards, passports, birth certificates) to identify individuals. Children, who presented minimal physical threat and couldn't reproduce, probably weren't cause for concern.

However, adolescents' physical development allowed them to commit acts of violence and bear children, triggering a need to distinguish between insiders and outsiders. Not coincidentally, the ability to obtain native-like abilities dissipates around this time, as it probably did then. Thus, erroneous grammar and a non-native accent functioned as mechanisms to recognize strangers and preclude dangers to group survival (Brown, 2000; Cohen, 2012).

Another possibility involves the usefulness of learning another language—or the lack thereof. Natural disasters have periodically created bottlenecks during which human populations were significantly reduced. Already small groups became even less likely to encounter peoples who didn't speak their language. As humans shifted from hunting and gathering to farming thousands of years ago, an estimated five million people lived on the entire earth. In such a world, a facility for learning another language like a native would have presented few survival advantages (Hagen, 2008).

THE ADVANTAGES OF BEING AN ADULT LANGUAGE LEARNER

Regardless of the causes of this uniquely human drama, the story isn't all bad for adults, nor is it uniformly positive for children. In fact, adults have many advantages over children, such as "more developed cognitive systems," a facility to construct "higher order associations and generalizations," and the ability to utilize "long-term memory rather than the short-term memory function used by children for rote learning" (Schleppegrell, 1987, para. 10).

If children leave the bilingual environment, they rarely possess the initiative and skill to continue studying the target language (Lightbown & Spada, 2013). Likewise, adults can learn the grammar of foreign languages faster than children, and strong motivation—in addition to immersion in the target language, accepting one's pronunciation level, and minimizing feelings of inadequacy—may reduce the impact of biological limitations (Flege, 1987; Marinova-Todd, Marshall, & Snow, 2000). The children of immigrants, or heritage speakers, frequently speak with native-like pronunciation but have a restricted vocabulary and lack literacy skills (Polinsky, 2014).

As a heritage speaker of French, linguist Francois Grosjean explains that his English-centered education left him with inadequate reading and writing abilities in his father's native tongue: "I recall having to struggle for a long time to bring my written French up to par when I came back to

France at age eighteen, and even now I bless the developers of good French grammar and spell checkers!" (Grosjean, 2012, para. 6).

FEW ARE PERFECT, BUT MOST CAN BE PRETTY GOOD!

Skeptics might say, "Well, those heritage speakers don't *really* speak the language." Ironically, such statements often come from monolinguals! For them, accentless pronunciation, perfect grammar, and a huge vocabulary must be possessed to be considered truly bilingual. Francois Grosjean asserts that speaking two or more languages doesn't mean speaking them with the same proficiency, and "a very small minority, have equal and perfect fluency in their languages" (Grosjean, 2000, para. 3).

The late Pope John Paul II supposedly spoke eight languages "fluently." But that doesn't mean he spoke them like his native Polish. Videos show his English to be clear but with a heavy accent. While he was able to give speeches and engage foreign ambassadors in highly formal ceremonies with relative ease, it is unlikely he wouldn't have struggled during impromptu conversations about tax reform and diabetes in most of those eight languages. Even a renowned linguist frequently cited in this book, Zoltan Dörnyei, doesn't sound like a native speaker of English.

The mixing of both languages exhibited by heritage speakers doesn't end in confusion and is a common practice for bilinguals (Guiberson, 2013). In fact, most engage in two types of linguistic fusion: *code-mixing* and *code-switching*. The former involves the structures and meanings of one language influencing the other, while the latter comprises changing from one language to the other (Ayeomoni, 2006). *Bringar* (to bring) and *chompear* (to chomp) are examples of Spanish-English code-mixing. Here English words are used within a Spanish grammatical framework.

At Sunday brunch, the children of a bilingual family may use Spanish to discuss soccer, switch to English to confess unfinished homework, go back to Spanish when grandma calls, and end with English to ask permission to play video games. Code-mixing and code-switching can be caused by varying levels of domain knowledge in each language and/or perception of one's bilingual skills or those of interlocutors (Heredia & Altarriba, 2001; Shin & Milroy, 2000).

To be sure, exceptionally skilled bilinguals (and multilinguals) do emerge, but these individuals undergo intensive and extensive social and academic formation in both languages, something which not even most Europeans can claim. Former New Mexico governor and secretary of energy Bill Richardson was born in California but lived and studied in Mexico City and Massachusetts as a child (Achenbach, 2007). He passes as native in both languages.

Writer Francisco Goldman effortlessly gives interviews in Spanish and English. His Jewish American father and Guatemalan mother had a stormy marriage, which resulted in his formative years "spent 'bouncing' between Guatemala and a 'brutal' Irish-Italian suburb in Massachusetts" (Jaggi, 2008, para. 10). Playwright Ariel Dorfman experienced his youth in Argentina, the United States, and Chile, during which he encountered the richness of life in English and Spanish—a unique gift unknown to most people (Dorfman, 1998).

And there are some who seem to have a unique *aptitude* or ability to learn languages, which is "distinct from general intelligence and achievement" (Sheen, 2007, p. 259). As linguist Vivian Cook accurately points out, "everybody knows people who have a knack for learning second languages and others who are rather poor at it" (Cook, 2016, p. 162). Another linguist, Stephen Krashen, reported the story of a Mexican-born man, Armando, who possessed unusually good Hebrew skills, especially considering he never lived in Israel. Armando arrived in Los Angeles at seventeen and had been employed at an Israeli restaurant for twelve years when Krashen met him (Krashen, 2000).

His laid-back approach to learning Hebrew would probably cause the average person to harbor significant doubts about his Hebrew skills: "Armando told me that he had never learned to read Hebrew, never studied Hebrew grammar, had no idea of what the rules of Hebrew grammar were" (Krashen, 2000, p. 22). Krashen asked four native speakers of Hebrew to assess his speaking abilities, two of whom described him as a native speaker. Even though the average person in his situation may be able to achieve an advanced level of oral Hebrew, it seems doubtful they could pass as a native speaker.

Another remarkable adult learner of Hebrew was the writer and filmmaker Ephraim Kishon. A native of Budapest, Hungary, Kishon survived the Holocaust and arrived in Israel in his mid-twenties "knowing neither Yiddish nor Hebrew" (Joffe, 2005, para. 9), two of the country's most commonly spoken Jewish languages at the time. Within a few years, he became a newspaper columnist and began writing plays and novels—all in Hebrew. Even though he worked very hard, his rate of learning and profound depth of linguistic knowledge went beyond the achievements hard work alone could have offered.

Language aptitude tests also suggest that innate distinctions between learners are real, at least at the beginning level. Such measures have traditionally involved recognizing and remembering sounds, discerning the grammatical roles played by words, formulating grammar rules, and memorizing vocabulary (Wen, 2012). Problematically, they have proven unable to forecast growth at the intermediate and advanced levels (Robinson, 2005). In addition, questions on assessments of language aptitude focus on skills emphasized in school settings—as opposed to naturalistic ones—and by outdated instructional methods (Cook, 2016).

These issues notwithstanding, probably no more than a freakishly insignificant number of people would score off the charts in all areas of these aptitude tests. Those that can aren't like John Travolta's character in the film *Phenomenon*—a man who develops extraordinary abilities after a mysterious light descends on him one night while outside a bar. He goes on to learn Portuguese in less than half an hour (Boyle & Turtelaub, 1996)!

Nor do they reflect Kevin Costner's character in the 1980s spy thriller *No Way Out*. In this movie, US Navy Lieutenant Commander Tom Farrell is called to work for Defense Secretary David Brice. The married military chief has an affair with a woman known as Susan, whom Tom also loves. In a fit of rage, Brice accidentally kills Susan. Meanwhile, an internal investigation at the Pentagon is focused on finding a Russian mole named Yuri. At the end of the film, viewers discover Yuri is really Tom Farrell: no accent, no grammatical mistakes; just the California English spoken by Kevin Costner (Garland & Donaldson, 1987).

The phenoms described in this chapter and the last probably are as good as they get, and even they had shortcomings. Joseph Conrad, for example, spoke with a pronounced Polish accent (Grosjean, 2011), and the influence of Polish grammar in his English writing has been documented (Morzinski & Pauly, 2009). Samuel Beckett's choice of French was born out of a desire to compose uncomplicated works that avoided the verbosity of his early English poetry (Dewaele, 2007), which is clearly an admission of unequal knowledge of both languages. While two judges thought Armando was a native-born Israeli, another guessed he was Ethiopian, and a fourth suspected he was an immigrant who had studied Hebrew for a year or two (Krashen, 2000). Ephraim Kishon brilliantly satirized Israeli life in impeccable Hebrew, yet "he never managed to get rid of his Hungarian accent" (Green, 2005, para. 10). In short, having a strong language aptitude isn't synonymous with perfection.

To be sure, those who escape monolingualism will understand much more about language and culture than their monolingual peers, but they won't experience a leap of intelligence. Bilinguals do have an enriched memory and heightened ability to regulate attentional resources during tasks (Bialystok, Craik, & Luk, 2012). These benefits, if utilized, obviously can enhance academic success, but common sense and simple observation demonstrate that bilingualism itself won't transform Average Joe American into Albert Einstein or Stephen Hawking.

A FINAL THOUGHT

A final thought concerns where readers should focus their energy. Dwelling on limitations and wishing for abnormal abilities or those which exist only in movies lead to negativity and inaction. What sense does it make to live this way? Instead of focusing on what can't be done, readers should be inspired by the non-native speakers who have achieved greatness, such as Kishon, Conrad, and Beckett. Also inspiring are the millions of anonymous people here and across the globe who survive in their non-native language. An accent and imperfect grammar haven't prevented them from engaging in meaningful social interaction and building successful careers.

And many of them learned another language with far less pain than the reader might imagine. While the process is challenging and sometimes tiring, it need not be boring and perpetually anxiety-provoking. In the next chapter, readers will discover that comprehension and enjoyment are the two keys which open the door to oral and written development.

DISCUSSION QUESTIONS

1. Before reading this chapter, what did you think about the differences between child and adult language learners?

2. Think of an adult immigrant and a child immigrant you know. How does their English differ?
3. In your opinion, why don't we study languages like many European countries? How could we change this?
4. How has this chapter changed your language-learning goals?
5. How has this chapter changed the way you approach those goals?

RECOMMENDED READING

Konnikova, M. (2015, January 15). Is bilingualism really an advantage? *The New Yorker*. Retrieved from http://www.newyorker.com/science/maria-konnikova/bilingual-advantage-aging-brain

This newspaper article concisely summarizes the disputes about the benefits of bilingualism and provides links to key writings on the topic.

REFERENCES

Achenbach, J. (2007, May 21). The pro-familia candidate. *The Washington Post*. Retrieved from http://www.washingtonpost.com/wp-dyn/content/article/2007/05/20/AR2007052001407.html?hpid=topnews

Ayeomoni, M. (2006). Code-switching and code-mixing: Style of language use in childhood in Yoruba speech community. *Nordic Journal of African Studies, 15*, 90–99.

Bialystok, E., Craik, F., & Luk, G. (2012). Bilingualism: Consequences for mind and brain. *Trends in Cognitive Science, 16*, 240–250. doi: 10.1016/j.tics.2012.03.001

Birdsong, D., & Molis, M. (2001). On the evidence for maturational constraints in second-language acquisition. *Journal of Memory and Language, 44*, 235–249. doi:10.1006/jmla.2000.2750

Boyle, B. (Producer), & Turtelaub, J. (Director). (1996). *Phenomenon* [Motion picture]. United States: Buena Vista Pictures.

Brown, H. (2000). *Principles of language learning and teaching* (4th ed.). White Plains, NY: Pearson.

Cohen, E. (2012). The evolution of tag-based cooperation in humans: The case for accent. *Current Anthropology, 53*, 588–605. doi: 10.1086/667654

Cook, V. (2016). *Second language learning and language teaching* (5th ed.). New York: Routledge.

DeKeyser, R., & Larson-Hall, J. (2005). What does the critical period really mean? In J. Kroll & A. De Groot (Eds.), *Handbook of bilingualism: Psycholinguistic approaches* (pp. 88–108). New York: Oxford University Press.

Dewaele, J. (2007). Becoming bi- or multi-lingual later in life. In P. Auer & L. Wei (Eds.), *Handbook of multilingualism and multilingual communication* (pp. 89–118). Berlin: De Gruyter.

Dorfman, A. (1998, June 24). If only we all spoke two languages. *The New York Times.* Retrieved from http://www.nytimes.com/1998/06/24/opinion/if-only-we-all-spoke-two-languages.html

Education First. (2016). *EF English proficiency index.* Cambridge, MA: Author. Retrieved from http://www.ef.edu/epi/

Edwards, A. (2014). *English in the Netherlands: Functions, forms, and attitudes* (Unpublished doctoral dissertation). Cambridge, UK: University of Cambridge.

European Commission. (2012). *Europeans and their languages.* Retrieved from http://ec.europa.eu/commfrontoffice/publicopinion/archives/ebs/ebs_386_en.pdf

Fanton, J. (2017). *America's languages: Investing in language education for the 21st century.* Cambridge, MA: American Academy of Arts and Sciences. Retrieved from https://www.amacad.org/content/publications/publication.aspx?d=22474

Feinberg, R. (Reporter). (2016, October 26). Maine grapples with "crisis level" foreign language teacher shortage [Radio program]. In N. Flaherty [Producer], *Maine Things Considered.* Portland, ME: Maine Public. Retrieved from http://mainepublic.org/post/maine-grapples-crisis-level-foreign-language-teacher-shortage

Flege, J. (1987). A critical period for learning to pronounce foreign languages? *Applied Linguistics, 8,* 162–177. doi: 10.1093/applin/8.2.162

Flege, J., Yeni-Komshian, G., & Liu, S. (1999). Age constraints on second language acquisition. *Journal of Memory and Language, 41,* 78–104. doi: 10.1006/jmla.1999.2638

Friedmann, N., & Rusou, D. (2015). Critical period for first language: The crucial role of language input during the first year of life. *Current Opinion in Neurobiology, 35,* 27–34.

Garland, R. (Producer), & Donaldson, R. (Director). (1987). *No way out* [Motion picture]. United States: MGM.

Goldberg, D., Looney, D., & Lusin, N. (2015). *Enrollments in languages other than English in United States institutions of higher education, fall 2013.* New York: Modern Language Association. Retrieved from https://www.mla.org/content/download/31180/1452509/EMB_enrllmnts_nonEngl_2013.pdf

Green, S. (2005, January 31). He captured Hebrew—and Hebrew captured him. *Haaretz.* Retrieved from https://www.haaretz.com/israel-news/culture/1.4719539

Grosjean, F. (2000, March 26). *Myths about bilingualism.* Retrieved from http://www.francoisgrosjean.ch/myths_en.html

Grosjean, F. (2011, January 25). Bilinguals and accents: Most bilinguals have an accent in one of their languages [Blog post]. Retrieved from https://www.psychologytoday.com/us/blog/life-bilingual/201101/bilinguals-and-accents

Grosjean, F. (2012, March 15). Portraying heritage language speakers: Heritage language speakers are bilinguals with a difference [Blog post]. Retrieved from https://www.psychologytoday.com/blog/life-bilingual/201203/portraying-heritage-language-speakers

Guiberson, M. (2013). Language confusion in bilingual children. *Perspectives on Communication Disorders and Sciences in Culturally and Linguistically Diverse Populations, 20,* 5–34. doi:10.1044/cds20.1.5

Hagen, L. (2008). The bilingual brain: Human evolution and second language acquisition. *Evolutionary Psychology, 6,* 43–63. doi: 10.1177/147470490800600105

Hakuta, K., Bialystok, E., & Wiley, E. (2003). Critical evidence: A test of the critical-period hypothesis for second-language acquisition. *Psychological Science, 14,* 31–38. doi: 10.1111/1467-9280.01415

Heredia, R., & Altarriba, J. (2001). Bilingual language mixing: Why do bilinguals code-switch? *Current Directions in Psychological Science, 10,* 164–168. doi: 10.1111/1467-8721.00140

Horwitz, E. (1988). The beliefs about language learning of beginning university foreign language students. *The Modern Language Journal, 72,* 283–294. doi: 10.1111/j.1540-4781.1988.tb04190.x

Jaggi, M. (2008, February 1). A path in the darkness. *The Guardian.* Retrieved from https://www.theguardian.com/books/2008/feb/02/featuresreviews.guardianreview12

Jha, A. (2011, March 28). China poised to overhaul US as biggest publisher of scientific papers. *The Guardian.* Retrieved from https://www.theguardian.com/science/2011/mar/28/china-us-publisher-scientific-papers

Joffe, L. (2005, January 31). Ephraim Kishon: Playwright and novelist whose satires shaped Israel's social agenda. *The Guardian.* Retrieved from https://www.theguardian.com/news/2005/feb/01/guardianobituaries.booksobituaries

Johnson, J., & Newport, E. (1989). Critical period effects in second language acquisition: The influence of maturational state on the acquisition of English as a second language. *Cognitive Psychology, 21,* 60–99. doi: 10.1016/0010-0285(89)90003-0

Jones, J. (2013, August 9). "Most in U.S. say it's essential that immigrants learn English." June 13–July 5, in *Gallup Politics.* Retrieved from http://www.gallup.com/poll/163895/say-essential-immigrants-learn-english.aspx

Kohli, S. (2014, December 10). A case for cutting foreign languages from US schools. *Quartz.* Retrieved from https://qz.com/309143/a-case-for-cutting-foreign-languages-from-us-schools/

Krashen, S. (2000). What does it take to acquire language? *ESL Magazine, 3*(3), 22–23. Retrieved from http://www.sdkrashen.com/content/articles/what_does_it_take.pdf

Language instruction in elementary and secondary schools. (2017, January). *Humanities Indicators.* Retrieved from http://www.humanitiesindicators.org/content/indicatorDoc.aspx?d=26&hl=englis h&m=I

Latomaa, S. (1998). English in contact with "the most difficult language in the world": The linguistic situation of Americans living in Finland. *International Journal of the Sociology of Language, 133,* 51–72. doi: 10.1515/ijsl.1998.133.51

Le, J. (2004). *Affective characteristics of American students studying Chinese in China: A study of heritage and non-heritage learners' beliefs and foreign language anxiety* (Unpublished doctoral dissertation). University of Texas, Austin, Texas.

Lightbown, P., & Spada, N. (2013). *How languages are learned* (4th ed.). New York: Oxford University Press.

Marinova-Todd, S., Marshall, D., & Snow, C. (2000). Three misconceptions about age and L2 learning. *TESOL Quarterly, 34,* 9–34. doi:10.2307/3588095

Mayberry, R., & Kluender, R. (2018). Rethinking the critical period for language: New insights into an old question from American Sign Language. *Bilingualism: Language and Cognition, 21,* 886–905. doi: 10.1017/S1366728917000724

Morzinski, M., & Pauly, V. (2009). Language. In A. Simmons (Ed.), *Joseph Conrad in context.* New York: Cambridge University Press.

Neeley, T. (2012, May). Global business speaks English. *Harvard Business Review.* Retrieved from https://hbr.org/2012/05/global-business-speaks-english

Polinsky, M. (2014). *Heritage languages and their speakers: Looking ahead.* Retrieved from http://nrs.harvard.edu/urn-3:HUL.InstRepos:33946918

Rifkin, B. (2000). Revisiting beliefs about foreign language learning. *Foreign Language Annals, 33,* 394–420. doi: 10.1111/j.1944-9720.2000.tb00621.x

Robinson, P. (2005). Aptitude and second language acquisition. *Annual Review of Applied Linguistics, 25,* 46–73. doi:10.1017/S0267190505000036

Schleppegrell, M. (1987). *The older language learner* (Report No. ED287313). ERIC Clearinghouse on Languages and Linguistics. Retrieved from http://ncu.libanswers.com/faq/190220

Schouten, A. (2009). The critical period hypothesis: Support, challenge, and reconceptualization. *Colombia University, Working Papers in TESOL & Applied Linguistics, 9*(1), 1–16.

Scovel, T. (2000). A critical review of the critical period research. *Annual Review of Applied Linguistics, 20,* 213–223. doi: 10.1017/S0267190500200135

Sheen, Y. (2007). The effect of focused written corrective feedback and language aptitude on ESL learners' acquisition of articles. *TESOL Quarterly, 41,* 255–283. doi: 10.1002/j.1545-7249.2007.tb00059.x

Shin, S., & Milroy, L. (2000). Conversational codeswitching among Korean-English bilingual children. *International Journal of Bilingualism, 4,* 351–383. doi: 10.1177/13670069000040030401

Simpson, M. (2007). From savage to citizen: Education, colonialism and idiocy. *British Journal of Sociology of Education, 28,* 561–574. doi: 10.1080/01425690701505326

Skorton, D., & Altschuler, G. (2012, August 27). America's foreign language deficit. *Forbes.* Retrieved from https://www.forbes.com/sites/collegeprose/2012/08/27/americas-foreign-language-deficit/#149f66684ddc

Steward, D. (2006). The foreign language requirement in English doctoral programs. *Profession, 16,* 203–218. doi: 10.1632/prof.2006.2006.1.203

Wen, Z. (2012). Foreign language aptitude. *ELT Journal, 66,* 233–235. doi:10.1093/elt/ccr068

3

COMPREHENSION AND ENJOYMENT: THE KEYS TO ACQUIRING GRAMMAR AND VOCABULARY

Particularly inspiring are the scores of immigrants who have arrived in the United States with no command of the English language. After a few years, many establish careers, start families, and develop some proficiency in English. Learning a new language and culture while working and raising a family is an enormous challenge. While postpubescent language learning doesn't require magical powers, it demands time and effort. Learners must engage the language on a daily basis and struggle through conversations and texts. The depth and breadth of linguistic knowledge they and other language learners obtain often depends on their goals.

Many feel content with producing everyday speech and possessing rudimentary literacy skills. Offering greetings, chitchatting about last night's basketball game, and asking about a café's lunch special could form the extent of their conversational needs. An ability to read street signs and fill out a job application for restaurant work may suffice. Such learners seek *Basic Interpersonal Communication Skills* (BICS). Coined by linguist Jim Cummins in the late 1970s, this term refers to language which takes roughly two years to learn (Roessingh, 2006).

A limited range of structures defines BICS, as does highly contextualized and concrete vocabulary. A learner able to use a couple thousand words can reasonably claim to hold BICS (Roessingh, 2006). While these accomplishments may seem unimpressive, they create a functional language user. A college student with BICS in French could fly unaccompanied to Paris, hail a cab, check into a hotel, and order room service. The next day, she could find her way to the metro, purchase a day pass from the clerk, and spend the day visiting museums. Local tourist literature would be comprehensible.

However, if a native Parisian engaged her in conversations about complex issues like US foreign policy, the literature of Marcel Proust, and her views on life after death, she would struggle. If the same person invited her to participate in a book club focused on critical theory, theoretical physics, or the history of French democracy, she would understand very little of what she read and heard. A request by one book club member to explain the gist of a recent American bestseller would likely yield a few words and long pauses but a negligible exchange of information.

Comprehending and using the grammatically complex and lexically rich language embedded in such situations requires *Cognitive Academic Language Proficiency* (CALP). Content knowledge, an ability to read and compose different types of texts, and a robust vocabulary all form part of CALP. Although education in the first language can impact the rate of CALP development, it typically emerges within five to seven years, often within the context of a formal academic setting (Cummins, 1980, 2008).

Much of this time is spent learning words, the understanding of which is indispensable for deep textual engagement (Schmitt, 2008). University students and those working in white-collar professions often read thousands of words daily; therefore, it is hardly surprising that "most researchers agree that vocabulary is a good predictor of reading, if not the best" (Laufer & Ravenhorst-Kalovski, 2010, p. 16). Such a generalization applies to both first and additional languages (Grabe, 2004).

BICS often precedes CALP, yet ignorance of the former need not preclude developing aspects of the latter. A scholar of the Protestant Reformation, for example, would find reading the original German writings of Martin Luther crucial for research purposes. He might cite them in scholarly publications and perhaps produce English translations of entire works. A simple conversation about Germany's World Cup performance or his feelings about a sibling's spouse, however, could prove extremely challenging, or even impossible.

Furthermore, readers shouldn't assume BICS lacks linguistic challenges. Idiomatic expressions, for example, normally make no literal sense. *It cost me an arm and a leg* can confuse non-native speakers, as can its Spanish equivalent, *me costó un ojo de la cara* (it cost me an eye from the face). Phrasal verbs, which meld transitive verbs with prepositions, often have multiple meanings (Larsen-Freeman, 1991; Side, 1990). *To go off* can indicate a lost temper, a deviation from correct behavior, and activation of something. *I went off on my dad*, *he went off the rails*, and *the bomb went off* all contain the same verb forms, yet their meanings are distinct.

GRAMMAR AND VOCABULARY: THE CORE OF BICS AND CALP

The centrality of grammar and vocabulary in BICS and CALP should now be obvious. Long before Cummins coined these terms, traditional instruction had prescribed ways of learning words and structures, one of the oldest being the aptly named *Grammar-Translation Method*, or GTM. Developed to foster translation abilities, it takes a *deductive approach* to grammar teaching and learning. In an average grammar lesson, the teacher presents various grammar rules and then exemplifies them in written form. Students memorize such rules and attempt to use them correctly in textbook exercises (Celce-Murcia, 1991; Richards & Rodgers, 2014).

A lesson on the present tense of the two Spanish *to be* verbs—*ser* and *estar*—might begin with an explanation—in the students' native language—of the circumstances under which to use both forms. The teacher would provide contrasting sentences with each verb, followed by oral justifications of his choices. To solidify knowledge of these rules, students could supply the correct verb forms in several fill-in-the-blank sentences. Tables containing usage and form rules would guide students in completing these exercises.

GTM also endorses memorization of vocabulary items "through bilingual word lists, dictionary study, and memorization" (Richards & Rodgers, 2014, p. 6). Often academic in nature, the meanings of these words are discussed and debated in students' native language. Vocabulary tests and translation exercises indicate students' mastery of them. Such tests often also require analysis and explanation of grammar rules yet ignore oral development.

The Audiolingual Method (ALM) also values repeating and memorizing vocabulary; unlike GTM, exercises principally use an oral format. Students listen to and repeat individual sentences and short dialogues in which specific grammatical structures are embedded, leading them to "an intuitive understanding of the rule" (Nunan, 2005, p. 15). ALM thus represents an *inductive approach* to grammar teaching and learning. The following dialogue between teachers and students aims at mastery of the linking verb *to be* (King & Campbell, 1955, p. 12):

Good morning, Mr. Martin.

–Good morning, Miss Andrade. Are you a student here?

Yes, I am. Are you a student, too?

–Yes, I am. And that's Mr. Grey.

Is he the teacher?

–No. He's a student.

Language learning in ALM represents just another human habit which is developed through activating stimuli and correctly responding to it, often repeatedly. Both ALM and GTM remain attractive to teachers, students, and parents because of their predictability, ease of planning, and lack of anxiety-inducing obligations to spontaneously speak the target language (Sapargul & Sartor, 2010). They also provide learners with a structural foundation, basic vocabulary, and often some notion of how to pronounce individual words.

However, the activities promoted by GTM and ALM should not dominate the language-learning repertoire of those independently developing BICS and CALP. Inside the classroom, students have long complained of the boredom that constant memorization, drilling, and repetition produce (Richards & Rodgers, 2014). Outside the classroom, evidence of similar feelings is abundant. Literary critic and translator Ilan Stavans provides one example. He endeavored to teach himself English by reading *Moby Dick* and looking up each unfamiliar word. Later, he "would read the segment again and repeat the list from memory. Obviously, this was a nightmarish approach" (Stavans, 2007, p. 132).

GRAMMAR: A BIG TENT

Syntax and Morphology

ALM and GTM texts also present learners with a simplistic notion of grammar: it is a finite set of identifiable rules contained in this book and perhaps a few others. The reality of grammar, however, involves complexity understood by few. All sentences—even those which are very short—contain *syntax* and *morphology*. The former refers to word order. In English, subjects come first, followed by verbs and direct objects (SVO). In the sentence *I hate cupcakes*, *I* is the subject, *hate* is the verb, and *cupcakes* is the direct object.

Other languages begin with verbs followed by subjects and direct objects, or they utilize a pattern of direct object + verb + subject. The most commonly studied language in the United States, Spanish, utilizes an SVO pattern, but it also allows for objects to sometimes precede verbs. In formal Arabic, the verb typically starts a sentence and is followed by the subject and object, respectively. Korean sentences place the subject first, the object after it, and the verb at the end (Swan & Smith, 2001).

Morphology refers to the parts of words. *Inflectional morphemes* are affixes which change aspects of a word without altering its grammatical function. For example: The suffix *-ED-* identifies the past tense, while *-S-* signifies the third-person singular present tense, and *-ING-* indicates the present progressive tense. Whatever verb they join remains a verb. Utterances like *She hates cupcakes*, *She is hating cupcakes,* and *She hated cupcakes* refer to different points in time, yet the word *hate* is a verb in all three clauses (Görlach, 1997).

Derivational morphemes, in contrast, transform a word's grammatical function. Verbs can become nouns, nouns can become verbs, and adjectives can become nouns, among other changes. *Person* is a noun that becomes an adverb when *-ALLY-* is attached (e.g., "He is a *person*" vs. "I *personally* don't like him"). The verb *devote* takes the function of a noun when *-TION-* is added (e.g., "I *devote* time to you" vs. "My *devotion* is great"). Another verb, *sense*, behaves as an adjective following the appearance of *-IBLE-* ("I *sense* you are mad" vs. "You are a *sensible* person") (Görlach, 1997).

Both inflectional and derivational morphemes are *bound morphemes* (i.e., morphemes without inherent meaning) which must join *free mor-*

phemes, which function as adjectives, adverbs, verbs, and nouns. *Cool* (adj.), *hard* (adv.), *eat* (v), and *apple* (n) are examples of free morphemes (Blachowicz & Fisher, 1996). In practice, joining free and bound morphemes can prove challenging. Readers who struggle with Spanish may recall the frustrating morphological changes verbs make to indicate uncertain and hypothetical situations (e.g., *Tú tomas agua*—"You drink water"—vs. *Yo quiero que tú tomes agua*—"I want you to drink water").

Prescriptive and Descriptive Grammar

Morphemes and syntax may differ depending on whether grammar is *prescriptive* or *descriptive*. Also referred to as *school grammar*, prescriptive grammar presents itself authoritatively, firmly establishing "what is correct or incorrect" (Greenbaum, 1996, p. 24). Mandates against splitting infinitives (e.g., *to really want*), ending sentences with prepositions (e.g., *What time is it at?*), putting yourself before others in sentences (e.g., *I and John want*), and using double negatives (e.g., *It don't matter none*) represent a few of the prescriptive rules known to the average educated American.

The emergence of prescriptive grammar, at least in English, was relatively recent. For most of European history, literacy and standards of linguistic usage revolved around Latin, not vernacular languages. Greek and Latin texts formed the core of university education, and thus the schools which educated the sons of the elite devoted much energy toward mastering these languages. Until the Protestant Reformation, religious services were held in Latin, the official language of the Roman Catholic Church. Laws and government edicts also utilized Latin (Gibson, 1989; Johnson, 2016).

For a variety of reasons, Latin's influence declined, while the use of vernaculars increased. In multidialectal Britain, this sparked concerns about the quality of grammar, vocabulary, and spelling in printed texts and school curricula, leading to calls for standardization and the subsequent birth of prescriptive English grammar. Unsurprisingly, much of this prescriptive grammar found its foundation in Latin and dialects spoken by eighteenth-century London-based aristocrats (Cipollone, Keiser, & Vasishth, 1998; Pinker, 1994).

Critics have long highlighted the artificial nature of prescriptive grammar, especially the disconnect between idealized rules and actual usage.

In addition, its elevation of dialects spoken by socioeconomic elites and stigmatization of those used by the poor and ethnic minorities are linguistically arbitrary and reinforce inequality (McWhorter, 2001). Nevertheless, it remains powerful. Surprisingly, the English-speaking world doesn't have quasigovernmental organizations that publish prescriptive grammars, like the Académie française (French) and Asociación de Academias de la Lengua Española (Spanish) (Stavans, 2013).

Such authoritarianism is lacking from descriptive grammar, which "describes it as it is, not as it should be" (Bourke, 2005, p. 88). "It" refers to the constructions speakers formulate and the social conditions under which they do so. The contexts in which double negatives appear, gender differences in the use of adjectives, and verb constructions in Appalachia are a few examples of research which interests descriptive grammarians. While this grammar is ridiculed or ignored in prescriptive texts, it forms a large part of everyday speech in all languages (Stamper, 2017).

The Inconsistency of Rules

Language learners quickly notice the inconsistency of rules in both descriptive and prescriptive grammar. In English, constructing the past and present progressive tenses normally requires adding -*ED*- and -*ING*-, respectively, to the end of verbs. Students of Biblical Hebrew are taught plural feminine nouns have the suffix -*OT*-, while masculine plural nouns have -*IM*-. Their Spanish-learning peers also discover morphological differences between feminine (-*A*-) and masculine (-*O*-) nouns and the indefinite (*un/una*) and definite (*la, el*) articles which precede them.

However, many English verbs shun the regular past tense ending and communicate time shifts through vowel changes (e.g., *fall* vs. *fell*; *forbid* vs. *forbade*; *get* vs. *got*) and entirely different words (e.g., *go* vs. *went*; *am* vs. *was*). One of the most frequently used words in Biblical Hebrew, *avot* (fathers), utilizes the feminine ending, and scores of Spanish nouns ending in -*A*- are masculine instead of feminine, such as *el clima* (climate) and *el mapa* (map). These examples demonstrate any approach that "encourages the belief that learning a language is simply a case of knowing the rules" (Thornbury, 1999, p. 30) clearly isn't telling the whole story.

The Richness of Vocabulary

Prescriptive and descriptive grammar contains thousands of words, the richness of which receives little consideration in the Grammar-Translation and Audiolingual Methods. Individual terms frequently possess a multiplicity of definitions. The word *pool,* for example, refers to a natural or artificial body of water, a game in which players hit balls into holes on a felt-covered table, a group of applicants for a job or entry into a university, and a collection of money or resources. *Bark* is material that grows on tree exteriors, a semihard candy that contains chocolate or vanilla, and a noise dogs create when hungry or disturbed.

The *denotations* of words—that is, the literal meaning frequently found in dictionaries—often differ from their *connotations*, which "show people's emotions and attitudes towards what the word or phrase refers to" (Richards, Platt, & Platt, 1992, p. 78). Verbatim translation can lead to communication breakdowns, some of which can have dire consequences. Two words, *stupid* and *fat*, have radically different emotional voltage levels in American English and Colombian Spanish.

In American English, a friend's self-doubt about his attractiveness and intelligence can earn the reply *don't be stupid*, the intention of which is to assuage worries and boost self-esteem. In Colombian Spanish, however, labeling an interlocutor's feelings as *stupid* constitutes an insult. On the other hand, an American who calls a friend *fat* upon meeting after a long period of physical separation can seem cruel and may have just destroyed a relationship; the same comment in Colombian Spanish—*estás gordito*—may reflect a simple observation and evoke minor irritation, at most.

In addition to the boredom triggered by memorizing such distinctions, the process of selecting words and grammar to study, as well as finding pedagogical materials that address them, would consume an impractical amount of time. Remembering word forms and usages and learning syntactical and morphological rules would cause cognitive overload and quickly lead to exhaustion. Outside of formal instructional settings, such activities produce irritable linguistic drop-outs and perpetuate monolingualism. Alternatively, practices which supply *comprehensible input* (CI) can build the grammar and vocabulary for BICS and CALP.

COMPREHENSIBLE INPUT

CI in the First Language

Before detailing CI in foreign-language learning, its role in developing the first language merits attention. Contrary to the views of psychologists in the first half of the twentieth century, scientists now realize children possess an innate grammatical blueprint which facilitates language growth. To produce a functional grammar, it requires environmental linguistic stimuli which doesn't rely on mindless repetition, drills, memorization, and explicit understanding of rules (Chomsky, 1959).

Instead, such stimuli come as words and phrases related to feelings, actions, and visual elements in childhood environments. This language "is a little beyond our current level of competence" yet can be understood "with the aid of extra-linguistic context or our knowledge of the world" (Krashen, 1981, p. 103). Also known as *motherese*, it principally comes from parents and other primary caregivers (Fernald, 1985).

CI in the Foreign Language

Individual words, phrases, and clauses slowly emerge because of this input. This process is known as *language acquisition*. Also available to foreign-language learners, acquisition builds knowledge of words and grammatical patterns while avoiding the boredom and fatigue involved in memorization, repetition, and drilling (Krashen & Terrell, 1998). As in the first language, acquisition is subconscious, and learners "are not usually aware of the fact that they are acquiring language, but are only aware of the fact that they are using the language for communication. The result of language acquisition, acquired competence, is also subconscious" (Krashen, 1982, p. 10).

Obviously, older learners cannot re-experience their childhood and face limitations because of the critical period. However, they can likely still access an innate linguistic blueprint, and their autonomy allows them to seek comprehensible input and acquire a language independently. *Free voluntary reading* represents one way of doing this. When language learners engage written materials familiar to them and not too far beyond their current proficiency, they acquire grammar and vocabulary (Krashen, 2004; Rodrigo, 2003).

These texts should focus on appealing areas: romance, politics, history, sports, and wellness are all on the table. Readers' understanding of these topics facilitates comprehension and subsequent acquisition of grammar and vocabulary (Krashen, 1997). Harry Potter fans' granular knowledge of the novels can help them acquire French or Spanish when they read them in translation. Years of Star Wars fandom and pictures that accompany dialogue make a Luke Skywalker comic book comprehensible.

A regular reader of *National Geographic* can access translations in a number of languages. After reading articles in English, words and phrases previously unknown would make sense in translation. An online news junky could read an article in English about a natural disaster to provide a base for a French-language report on the same topic. A Ronaldo-obsessed soccer player might utilize familiarity with his life and the sport to understand Portuguese-language articles about controversial matches and his activities off the field. In a previous publication, Poole (2011) described how his love of James Bond films facilitated comprehension of Spanish-language 007 novels.

Research has shown the positive influence of free voluntary reading on BICS. In one classic study, researchers worked with a group of four immigrant women (three Korean, one Spanish-speaking), only one of whom felt sufficiently confident to regularly communicate with native speakers of English. To improve their English, they were introduced to the Sweet Valley Kids series, which focuses on a set of elementary-aged twins. The books aim to entertain and doubtfully would form part of a language-arts curriculum (Cho & Krashen,1994).

The participants quickly developed sustained engagement with these stories and read between eight and twenty-three individual novels. Tests of vocabulary development showed marked progress, with word additions between 7.1 and 37.4 per volume. More interesting, however, are the self-reported expansions of their oral comprehension and productive abilities. One participant noted that prior to her participation in the study, she felt uncomfortable talking to Americans, "but the other day when I went to Disneyland, I enjoyed talked [*sic*] to some American children and their parents who came from Arizona" (Cho & Krashen, 1994, p. 666).

Research has also demonstrated the positive influence of free voluntary reading on CALP. Beniko Mason and Stephen Krashen examined the impact of young adult literature series (e.g., Harry Potter, Twilight) on eight Japanese adults' scores on the Test of English for International Communications (TOEIC), a standardized exam focusing on reading and listening. Participants read between 22 and 162 weeks (Mason & Krashen, 2017).

Scores increased for all students; on average, an hour of reading led to slightly more than a half point (.6) increase in test scores. With such gains, the authors concluded that "a reader can move from the bottom of the 'Elementary Proficiency' level to the threshold of the 'International Proficiency' in three years of relaxed, self-selected pleasure reading" (Mason & Krashen, 2017, p. 474).

Even messing around on the internet, which Stephen Krashen has termed *free voluntary web-surfing*, can furnish comprehensible input (Krashen, 2011). He cautions that learners should have the ability to read basic texts (e.g., news reports) in the target language. Fun, personally enriching websites are ideal; serious, work-related websites should be avoided. Learners might put forth significant energy locating the right sites, so patience is required. Ideally, however, learners will find them so captivating they will lack awareness of the text's foreignness.

Comprehensible input doesn't limit itself to written products. Learners can watch dubbed versions of Harry Potter movies and National Geographic programs. Satellite television and streaming services provide access to soccer games in Spanish, French, German, Italian, Portuguese, and a number of non-European languages. Podcasts offer listening possibilities unthinkable a decade ago. Topics range from news and sports to religion, history, and entertainment.

These aural resources enable *narrow listening*, which involves listening to a program on the same topic several times. Repeated listening allows learners to hear parts missed due to distractions or difficulties following rapid speech. In conjunction with knowledge of and enthusiasm about a topic, this activity can create conditions for acquisition. Learners should vary topics and can even interview native speakers for later listening (Krashen, 1996).

Beatrice Dupuy utilized narrow listening with her beginning and intermediate students of French at an American university. Native speakers of French made short recordings (one to two minutes) on a variety of topics. Many participants listened to the tapes several times, and most reported their listening improved. They felt the experience was worthwhile and gave them more confidence in their receptive abilities (Dupuy, 1999).

Combining narrow listening with *narrow reading* (i.e., reading texts on a single topic) has even been suggested because it can reduce processing demands and provide even more context for grammar and vocabulary acquisition. In one Japanese university program, low-intermediate students watched the film *Hotel Rwanda* and read essays about the genocide the movie dramatizes. The students encountered the same words and phrases in written and aural format, which aided their oral production of them (Kimura & Ssali, 2009). There is nothing to preclude learners from independently doing something similar.

A FINAL THOUGHT

In sum, reading and listening often provide input which leads to language acquisition. As seen in chapter 1, these materials also often are motivating. However, finding them can be difficult, especially in numerically small languages and those without literacy. Discovering interesting books, magazines, and audio programs requires trial and error. It may also involve losing money. Resources which initially appear attractive may prove too difficult, absurdly easy, or just plain boring. This reality might discourage some readers, but it shouldn't. Monolinguals and multilinguals have the same problems. Why would first-time language learners escape them?

The reactions of others can prove more challenging. In American culture, effective learning is synonymous with overcoming difficulties. Good students must always sacrifice and suffer. Monolingual peers, parents, and other adults may dismiss the fan fiction learners read and online videos they watch as entertainment, not serious study. Advice—much of it uninformed by research or experience—will probably follow this condemnation. In short, learners should plan to feel irritated.

Finally, comprehensible input doesn't eliminate all frustration from the actual learning process. Errors will still happen. Production which is always form-precise and functionally accurate eludes all learners, especially at the beginning and intermediate levels. The next chapter details the causes of such roadblocks, emphasizes their integrality to language learning, and suggests steps to ameliorate their effects.

DISCUSSION QUESTIONS

1. Which is more challenging for you in the target language: BICS or CALP? Explain.
2. How do memorizing vocabulary words and analyzing grammar rules make you feel about language learning?
3. Do you think Americans view language learning as something which must be difficult and unpleasant? If so, why?
4. What types of materials interest you for free voluntary reading and listening?
5. Why is regular repetition of vocabulary words and grammar rules a problem while repeatedly listening to podcasts and books is beneficial?

RECOMMENDED READING

McQuillan, J. (2006). What can readers read after graded readers? *Reading in a Foreign Language, 28,* 63–78. Retrieved from https://files.eric.ed.gov/fulltext/EJ1098660.pdf.

McQuillan provides a roadmap for those considering implementing a regimen of free voluntary reading. He suggests types of texts for beginners and recommends criteria for selecting more challenging materials as proficiency increases.

REFERENCES

Blachowicz, C., & Fisher, P. (1996). *Teaching vocabulary in all classrooms.* Upper Saddle River, NJ: Prentice Hall.

Bourke, J. (2005). The grammar we teach. *Reflections on English Language Teaching, 4,* 85–97.

Celce-Murcia, M. (1991). Language teaching approaches: An overview. In M. Celce-Murcia (Ed.), *Teaching English as a second or foreign language* (2nd ed.) (pp. 3–10). Boston: Heinle & Heinle.

Cho, K., & Krashen, S. (1994). Acquisition of vocabulary from the Sweet Valley Kids series: Adult ESL acquisition. *Journal of Reading, 37,* 662–667.

Chomsky, N. (1959). Review of the book *Verbal behavior*, by B. F. Skinner. *Language, 35,* 26–58. doi: 10.2307/411334

Cipollone, N., Keiser, S., & Vasishth, S. (1998). *Language files: Materials for an introduction to language and linguistics* (7th ed.). Colombus: Ohio State University Press.

Cummins, J. (1980). The cross-lingual dimensions of language proficiency: Implications for bilingual education and the optimal age issue. *TESOL Quarterly, 14,* 175–187. Doi: 10.2307/3586312

Cummins, J. (2008). BICS and CALP: Empirical and theoretical status of the distinction. In B. Street & N. Hornberger (Eds.), *Encyclopedia of language and education* (2nd ed.) (pp. 71–83). New York: Springer Science + Business Media LLC.

Dupuy, B. (1999). Narrow listening: An alternative way to develop and enhance listening comprehension in students of French as a foreign language. *System, 27,* 351–361. doi: 10.1016/S0346-251X(99)00030-5

Fernald, A. (1985). Four-month-old infants prefer to listen to motherese. *Infant Behavior and Development, 8,* 181–195. doi: 10.1016/S0163-6383(85)80005-9

Gibson, J. (1989). Educating for silence: Renaissance women and the language arts. *Hypatia, 4,* 9–27. doi: 10.1111/j.1527-2001.1989.tb00865.x

Görlach, M. (1997). *The linguistic history of English.* London: Macmillan.

Grabe, W. (2004). Research on teaching reading. *Annual Review of Applied Linguistics, 24,* 44–69. doi: 10.1017/S0267190504000030

Greenbaum, S. (1996). *Oxford English grammar.* Oxford: Oxford University Press.

Johnson, K. (2016). *The history of early English: An activity-based approach.* New York: Routledge.

Kimura, H., & Ssali, V. (2009). The case for combining narrow reading and listening. *The Language Teacher, 33,* 9–13.

King, H., & Campbell, R. (1955). *Inglés al día* (2nd ed.). Bogotá, Colombia: Editorial Voluntad.

Krashen, S. (1981). *Second language acquisition and second language learning.* Oxford: Pergamon Press. Retrieved from http://www.sdkrashen.com/content/books/sl_acquisition_and_learning.pdf

Krashen, S. (1982). *Principles and practice in second language acquisition.* Oxford: Pergamon Press. Retrieved from http://www.sdkrashen.com/content/books/principles_and_practice.pdf

Krashen, S. (1996). The case for narrow listening. *System, 24,* 97–100. doi:10.1016/0346-251X(95)00054-N

Krashen, S. (1997). Free voluntary reading: It works for first language, second language, and foreign language acquisition. *MEXTESOL Journal, 20,* 11–18.

Krashen, S. (2004, April). *Free voluntary reading: New research, applications, and controversies.* Paper presented at RELC Conference, Singapore. Retrieved from http://www.sdkrashen.com/content/articles/singapore.pdf

Krashen, S. (2011). *Free voluntary reading.* Santa Barbara, CA: Libraries Unlimited.

Krashen, S., & Terrell, T. (1998). *The natural approach: Language acquisition in the classroom.* New York: Prentice Hall.

Larsen-Freeman, D. (1991). Teaching grammar. In M. Celce-Murcia (Ed.), *Teaching English as a second or foreign language* (2nd ed.) (pp. 279–295). Boston: Heinle & Heinle.

Laufer, B., & Ravenhorst-Kalovski, G. (2010). Lexical threshold revisited: Lexical text coverage, learners' vocabulary size and reading comprehension. *Reading in a Foreign Language, 22,* 15–30.

Mason, B., & Krashen, S. (2017). Self-selected reading and TOEIC performance: Evidence from case histories. *Shitennoji University Bulletin, 63,* 469–475.

McWhorter, J. (2001). *Word on the street: Debunking the myth of a "pure" standard English.* New York: Basic Books.

Nunan, D. (2005). *Grammar.* Boston: McGraw-Hill.

Pinker, S. (1994, January 31). Grammar puss: The fallacies of the language mavens. *The New Republic.* Retrieved from https://newrepublic.com/article/77732/grammar-puss-steven-pinker-language-william-safire

Poole, A. (2011). The monitor model and me. *The International Journal of Foreign Language Teaching, 7*(1), 13–16.

Richards, J., Platt, J., & Platt, H. (1992). *Dictionary of language teaching and applied linguistics* (2nd ed.). Harlow, UK: Longman.

Richards, J., & Rodgers, T. (2014). *Approaches and methods in language teaching* (3rd ed.). Cambridge: Cambridge University Press.

Rodrigo, V. (2003). Narrow listening and audio-library: The transitional stage in the process of developing listening comprehension in a foreign language. *MEXTESOL Journal,* 27, 9–25. Retrieved from http://mextesol.net/journal/public/files/6b516e6d0cdcc0fe6e58b8123fcc7b52.pdf

Roessingh, H. (2006). BICS-CALP: An introduction for some, a review for others. *TESL Canada Journal/ Revue TESL du Canada, 23,* 91–96. doi: 10.18806/tesl.v23i2.57

Sapargul, D., & Sartor, V. (2010). The trans-cultural comparative literature method: Using grammar translation techniques effectively. *English Teaching Forum, 48,* 26–33.

Schmitt, N. (2008). Review article: Instructed second language vocabulary learning. *Language Teaching Research, 12,* 329–363. doi: 10.1177/1362168808089921

Side, R. (1990). Phrasal verbs: Sorting them out. *ELT Journal, 44,* 144–152. doi: org/10.1093/elt/44.2.144

Stamper, K. (2017). *Word by word: The secret life of dictionaries.* New York: Pantheon Books.

Stavans, I. (2007). Amerika, America. In T. Miller (Ed.), *How I learned English: 55 accomplished Latinos recall lessons in language and life* (pp. 131–134). Washington, D.C.: National Geographic.

Stavans, I. (2013, December 16). Why doesn't English have an academy? *The Chronicle of Higher Education.* Retrieved from https://www.chronicle.com/blogs/linguafranca/2013/12/16/why-doesnt-english-have-an-academy/

Swan, M., & Smith, B. (2001). *Learner English: A teacher's guide to interference and other problems.* Cambridge: Cambridge University Press.

Thornbury, S. (1999). *How to teach grammar.* Harlow, UK: Pearson.

4

ERRORS: KEYS TO GETTING AHEAD

In light of the time required to develop BICS and CALP, most readers probably already doubt that comprehensible input automatically results in impeccable language production. Grammar indeed appears to marinate in the learner's head before presenting itself in speech. Something similar occurs with the first language. While children encounter language at birth, grammatical competence only arises after four or five years (Fromkin, Rodman, & Hyams, 2011).

While the stages involved in foreign-language learning are not totally understood, the emergence of language itself holds far more mystery. Caregiving precedes word formation, casting doubt on the idea that language is essential for human existence. Language likely trailed the emergence of the human species. Although dating both presents obvious archival challenges, 180,000 years ago is a reasonable estimate for the appearance of modern humans' earliest ancestor (Lewis, 2016). Language seems to have come thousands of years later (McWhorter, 2004).

It paralleled other cognitive developments, like tool making and visual art (Balter, 2015). Human physiology also transformed during this period. The brain grew, and vocal tracts which enabled production of sounds available to present-day humans developed (Jackendoff, 2006; Pinker, 2003). Linguistic output presumably developed in stages, with sounds and individual words initially functioning as symbols instead of grammatical components (Jackendoff, 1999).

Elegant explanations of the causal factors involved in linguistic evolution evade scientists. Some link language to natural selection, pointing out the survival benefits it granted to humans. Others feel grammar's inefficacy makes such an account improbable and view language as a "by-product of selection for other abilities or as a consequence of as-yet unknown laws of growth and form" (Pinker & Bloom, 1990, p. 707). For a time, scientists believed the *FOXP2* gene could unlock the mystery of language, yet recent research has cast doubt on its contribution to human speech (Saey, 2018).

LANGUAGE IS UNIQUE TO HUMANS

That language uniquely exists in humans, however, is beyond reasonable doubt. Animals live and die without the vocal apparatus and neuromechanisms which permit human articulation (Alex, 2018). The creativity of language is "virtually limitless with respect to its scope of expression" (Hauser, Chomsky, & Fitch, 2002, p. 1569), while animal communication systems "typically have at most a few dozen distinct calls, and they are used only to communicate immediate issues such as food, danger, threat, or reconciliation" (Jackendoff, 2006, p. 1).

One feature of language unavailable to animals is recursion, or the ability to nest structures of the same nature within each other (Hauser & Fitch, 2003). The sentence *The salmon [that Sammy prepared] ate a diet of other fish* contains two clauses, one in brackets. Recursion permits an infinite number of such clauses. While awkward, sentences such as the following are thus grammatically acceptable: *The salmon [that Sammy prepared] [that Mo caught][that Fran cleaned][that Maria washed][that Augie smoked] ate a diet of other fish.*

The absence of these abilities and physiological elements eliminates *Planet of the Apes* scenarios, although attempts have been made to teach chimps and gorillas language. Starting in the 1970s, researchers expressed optimism about primates' capacity to understand spoken language and use sign language. However, intensive, decades-long training resulted in abilities significantly inferior to those enjoyed by small children (Wynne, 2007).

THE DEVELOPMENT OF GRAMMAR

First-Language Processes

Even though animal communication studies receive more media attention, research on child language acquisition is no less interesting. A pioneer in this field was B. F. Skinner. Those who have taken an introductory psychology course will recall his association with *behaviorism*, an approach to psychology which attributes general human conduct to external rewards and punishments. In his 1957 classic *Verbal Behavior*, Skinner asserted language also results from environmental stimuli, specifically "through imitation, reinforcement, analogy, and similar processes" (Fromkin, Rodman, & Hyams, 2011, p. 325).

Noam Chomsky, a then young linguist at the Massachusetts Institute of Technology, published a now legendary analysis of Skinner's work that demonstrated the improbability of behaviorist depictions of first-language development. Imitation of the immediate environment would vary the quality and pace of linguistic growth. Behaviorism thus predicts the child who experiences intensive direct speech from caregivers and extensive interaction with siblings will follow a different developmental timeline than the child rarely addressed by adults and peers. In real life, however, they display few differences (Chomsky, 1959; Dabrowska, 2015).

A review of child language socialization in three cultures—Anglo-American middle class, Kalui (an ethnic group in Papua New Guinea), and Western Samoan—empirically refutes the role of imitation. Anglo-American parents verbally interact with offspring immediately following birth, simplify speech, and assist child language output. In contrast, Kalui and Western Samoan parents engage in less child-centered speech, infrequently modify their output, and avoid prompting nonadult output, or baby talk. In spite of these disparate linguistic practices, these cultures produce strikingly similar language users (Ochs & Schieffelin, 1984).

However, the language all children produce is vividly dissimilar from anything in their environment. While children often repeat individual words spoken by caregivers, their syntactic constructions frequently bear little resemblance to caregiver speech (Chomsky, 1959). As the older sister of many boys, the author's mother fondly remembers one particularly timid brother telling her *to fray me but don't fall me down*, instead of *pick me up, but don't drop me,* or another version with structures used by their older siblings and parents.

Behaviorism views error correction as the remedy for flawed utterances, which Chomsky claims is indefensible (Cook, 1985). Ignoring them, however, can seem blasphemous to parents. Protests often relay anecdotes about the effectiveness of error correction, stressing their son or daughter appropriately formed a certain structure only following extensive correction. For these parents, inaccurate expressions like *Mommy like picture?* eventually become *Did mommy like the picture?* thanks to a little help from mom and dad. Chomsky claims the duration of correction merely coincides with natural development but fails to alter it (Yule, 2006).

Short-term changes give the illusion that correction helps children, yet such changes don't always manifest following correction. In fact, multiple attempts to alter a child's speech may fail to induce even one target-like utterance. The following example of negation formation demonstrates a child's incapacity to even understand the correction:

Child: Nobody don't like me.

Mother: No, say "Nobody likes me."

Child: Nobody don't like me.

(Eight repetitions of this dialog)

Mother: No, now listen carefully; say "Nobody likes me."

Child: Oh! Nobody don't likes me. (as cited in Yule, 2006, p. 157).

The mother's persistence suggests dogmatic thinking about correction and an unawareness of the fixed stages of child language acquisition, which no amount of parental enthusiasm accelerates. A baby's mind starts processing language soon after birth and recognizes sound differences after one month. A couple of months later, she starts cooing and forms vowel sounds, followed by consonants. Babbling, or the formulation of "a number of different vowels and consonants, as well as combinations such as ba-ba-ba and ga-ga-ga" (Yule, 2006, p. 152), emerges around the seventh month.

Near her first birthday, she produces individual words that communicate a variety of mental states, the meanings of which may not be immediately obvious (Fromkin, Rodman, & Hyams, 2011; Pinker, 1996). When eating peas and carrots in her high chair, she may suddenly scream *sippy*, prompting parental retrieval of the object. Frowning and tossing it across the room signals dad's erroneous interpretation of her wishes. He carries out various actions until finally discovering his daughter merely wants him to admire the sippy cup's pretty colors.

By the second year of life, she is combining two-word utterances, which lack helping verbs (e.g., *to be*), articles (e.g., *a/an* and *the*), and verb endings indicating tense (e.g., *-ED-*). Six months later, she can join several words together (Fromkin, Rodman, & Hyams, 2011). Statements resemble actual sentences but still lack morphological aspects of adult language. These gradually emerge, starting with *-ING-*, followed by the plural *-S-*, *-ED-*, and the third-personal-singular present-tense suffix *-S-* (Yule, 2006).

By this time, she has learned about ten thousand words. Initial vocabulary reflects the immediate environment. Children normally *overextend* and *underextend* newly learned terms. The former refers to using a word outside of its appropriate meaning boundary, such as calling all elderly men *grandpa*. The latter involves failure to appropriately extend a term outside one context (e.g., utilizing *dog* for the household animal, but not those outside of it) (Fromkin, Rodman, & Hyams, 2011).

Universal Grammar

The disconnect between children's understanding and production of language can perplex caregivers. For Chomsky, this gap is natural since linguistic competence precedes linguistic performance. Moreover, the former maintains a certain purity, while the latter manifests imperfectly because of distractions, memory issues, strong emotions, and interruptions (Searle, 1972). An intrinsic linguistic faculty provides the foundation for all language. Chomsky calls this *Universal Grammar* (Yang, Crain, Berwick, Chomsky, & Bolhuis, 2017).

Universal Grammar, or UG, consists of a finite number of structures theoretically available to all children at birth. However, only those in a child's immediate environment will develop. This process has been compared to building a house: "All of the houses have the same floor plan, but the occupants have some choices to make. They can have carpet or hardwood floors, curtains or blinds" (Fromkin, Rodman, & Hyams, 2011, p. 124). Children in English-speaking and Japanese contexts develop either subject-verb-object or subject-object-verb word order; however, in theory both are available to any child.

The Foreign Language

While Chomsky's ideas have generated criticism, they have dominated the linguistic research paradigm for decades. Their application to foreign-language learning, especially Universal Grammar, forced linguists to seriously consider that cognitive mechanisms mediate instructional activities. A discouraging stance asserts the unavailability of Universal Grammar after the early teen years and the fundamentally distinct nature of foreign-language learning. Partial access to UG through the first language is another possibility. A third view claims learners can draw upon UG without facilitation from the first language (White, 2003).

The research on acquisition presented in the previous chapter suggests at least partial access to UG. The nature of errors (see below) further indicates both direct access to UG and some role for the first language. Another similarity between children and foreign-language learners concerns the acquisition of grammar. As discussed above, these stages are fixed for children. In the *Natural Order Hypothesis*, Stephen Krashen maintains acquisition also occurs "in a predictable order" for older learners (Krashen & Terrell, 1998, p. 28).

Learners of English, for example, acquire the progressive verb form (e.g., Alex is go*ing*), followed by plural nouns (e.g., book*s*), the copula *to be* (e.g., Alex *is* a teacher), auxiliary verbs (e.g., Alex *is* teaching), articles (e.g., Alex is *a* teacher; He is *the* teacher), irregular past-tense verb forms (e.g., Alex *was* a teacher), the regular past-tense verb form (e.g., Alex kick*ed* the ball), the third-person-singular present tense (e.g., Alex want*s* a bagel), and finally the possessive noun affix (e.g., The bagel*'s* crust was dry) (Krashen, 1982).

These stages form part of a learner's *interlanguage*. Coined in 1972 by Larry Selinker, interlanguage refers to "developing second language knowledge," which possesses features "of the learner's first language, characteristics of the second language, and some characteristics that seem to be very general and tend to occur in all or most interlanguage systems." Interlanguage is simultaneously "systematic" and "dynamic" (Lightbown & Spada, 2013, p. 220). In layperson's terms, many of these "characteristics" are simply just errors.

Errors

Foreign-language errors tend to attract more attention than their first-language counterparts, at least partially because adults generally have communicative obligations children lack. Purchasing food, renting an apartment, and applying for a job can't wait for stages of acquisition. The visibility of older learners' errors also distinguishes them from elementary-aged children who enter school without knowledge of the language of instruction and undergo a *silent period*, which describes the limited language production at the initial stages of exposure (Krashen, 2018a).

Instead of passively receiving the language, the learner is developing competence "via active listening, via intake" (Krashen, 1981, p. 111), which eventually emerges into rudimentary speaking abilities. The silent period can persist for several months and cause concerns of developmental delays among educators unfamiliar with first- and foreign-language research. Instead of reducing linguistic growth, it fosters it; unfortunately, most older language learners must bypass it.

In reality, total silence from children, either in the first or a foreign language, is rare. Just like children in their first language, foreign-language learners commit *developmental errors*. Such errors are naturally occurring, inaccurate utterances produced prior to the acquisition of structurally appropriate forms (Dulay & Burt, 1974). Learners of Spanish, for example, pass through five stages in their acquisition of the verbs *ser* and *estar*, two separate Spanish forms of the verb *to be*.

They first form sentences without either (e.g., *Filomena Colombiana). The verb *ser* incorrectly appears in the second stage when *estar* should be used (e.g., *Cesca *es* jugando). The third stage exhibits *estar* plus -*NDO*-, signaling the progressive tense (e.g., Luna *está* durmie*ndo*). In stage four, learners use *estar* to indicate location (e.g., Millicent *está* *en* el centro commercial). In stage five, *estar* surfaces to convey feelings (e.g., Walter *está* bravo) (Van Patten, 2010).

While errors often first manifest in spoken language, they also appear in written form. Patsy Lightbown and Nina Spada analyzed texts written by a native speaker of Chinese and a native speaker of French. While

English and French have similar morphological systems, native French speakers committed the same error as their Chinese counterparts: omission of the third-person -*S*- on singular present-tense verbs (e.g., *He like* to eat). English learners and their teachers can attest to the frequency and duration of this error by speakers of many different first languages (Lightbown & Spada, 2013).

Not all errors are universal, but rather find their origin in learners' first languages. These *transfer errors*—which aren't features of first-language development—often interfere with accurate production of the target language (Corder, 1981). English-speaking learners' difficulties with Spanish articles exemplify such interference. While Spanish often places the definite plural article before nouns, English tends to use personal pronouns to modify them. Native speakers of English might transfer this pattern to Spanish and produce an intelligible, but slightly odd, construction like *me quité mis zapatos* (I took off *my* shoes) instead of the normative *me quité los zapatos* (I took off *the* shoes).

Spanish speakers also transfer patterns of their language into English, especially concerning articles. English avoids placing articles before abstract nouns, especially in generalized contexts, and thus produces utterances such as *love is important* and *democracy is fragile*. In Spanish, however, a definite article typically precedes an abstract noun. Utterances such as *el amor es complicado* and *la democracia es frágil* represent normative Spanish but erroneously emerge as **the love is important* and **the democracy is fragile* when literally translated into English.

Correction and Language Acquisition

Although traditional methods of foreign-language teaching endorse it, students often demand it, and teachers regularly offer it, error correction doesn't erase transfer and developmental errors. Like first-language acquisition, foreign-language acquisition generally fails to positively respond to error correction. In addition to the natural stages of acquisition, linguist John Truscott maintains there are several reasons for this, the first of which involves identifying errors. In oral situations, few teachers possess such detailed grammatical knowledge, nor do they have the attentional resources needed to detect such errors, particularly in a crowded classroom full of diversions (Truscott, 1999).

However, teacher knowledge alone is not sufficient for successful correction. Novice educators quickly learn that "even when the teacher fully understands an error and presents what would seem to be a clear correction, the correction may fail because the student does not understand it" (Truscott, 1999, p. 439). Acquisitional unreadiness may explain this lack of reception, yet teachers cannot always determine students' stages of acquisition with respect to specific aspects of syntax and morphology. Correction which is unaligned with students' current levels may cause them to associate the practice with frustration.

Relatively short class periods obligate teachers to balance error correction with other facets of language teaching, leaving little opportunity to consider individual learners' developmental levels, in addition to optimal correction methods. Because of these other demands, correction may feel erratic. Correcting an error in one context, yet not in another, may generate further confusion and cause learners to distrust the practice (Truscott, 1999).

The final and most significant problem with correction concerns its connection with speaking gains. Many learners show no gains, while others exhibit temporary gains which decrease with time. Claims of success typically have limited assessment to correct usage in specific situations and ignored the problem of overusing newly encountered forms. Test performance in environments familiar to students (i.e., school) may not reflect the abilities of learners in real-life contexts (Truscott, 1999).

The evidence for the productivity of written grammar correction is similarly scant. Based on a review of relevant research, Truscott (2007) concluded that written correction, at most, fosters minor grammatical improvements, and can even result in decreased grammatical accuracy. Specifically, studies with controlled and experimental groups showed small effect sizes, while for those focused on overall improvements, "the best estimate is a negligible effect" (p. 267).

Is Learning Grammar a Waste of Time?

In spite of this evidence, a learning environment which bans correction seems rather extreme. Many students claim error correction, in addition to explicit grammar instruction, improved their grammar. While it almost certainly left acquisition unaltered, such correction likely did help them learn grammar rules and avoid errors. While *learning* is a general term used in this text and others to refer to the whole enterprise of studying another language, *learning grammar and vocabulary* means something very specific—and it differs from acquiring them. Learning vocabulary involves the memorization, repetition, and dictionary use discussed in chapter 3. Instead of absorbing grammar rules through comprehensible input, learning them involves explicit knowledge about morphology and syntax, which often doesn't smoothly translate to language production (Krashen, 2018b). Unlike small children acquiring their first language, foreign-language learners can amass an arsenal of rules. As discussed above, doing so entails many practical challenges (and limitations), in addition to spending significant amounts of time thinking about grammar. However, if learners willingly learn rules from correction and other forms of explicit grammar study, they can reap some benefits.

Specifically, such rules can compensate for breakdowns in the acquired system when learners are speaking and writing. This idea finds its clearest articulation in Stephen Krashen's *Monitor Hypothesis* (Krashen, 1982). Krashen claims learners possess an internal monitor that allows observing and editing language production. Thus, the learner of Spanish who utters *me quité mis zapatos* might use the monitor to notice the error and quickly reformulate it. Likewise, the French-speaking learner of English might use the monitor to edit a college paper. He would likely notice *he want, *he like, *he eat and similar constructions need an -*S*- at the end of the verb.

While the monitor may appear novel, it also develops in the first language. As in a foreign language, differences in the acquired and learned system also eventually emerge in the first language. In such cases, the monitor repairs erroneous language, especially in written form (Krashen, 2012). Pausing to remember distinctions between *its* and *it's* and stopping to reflect on past participle forms of irregular verbs (e.g., to see, to swim), for example, are actions familiar to most writers. In particularly lengthy sentences, the acquired system generates faulty sentence-verb agreement, which the monitor detects and corrects with learned grammar rules.

In the first language, monitoring mainly aids appropriateness, while in a foreign language, it promotes precision and clarity. However, its feasibility depends on three factors: time, understanding of rules, and learner attentiveness to form (Krashen, 1982). Learners must be allowed the opportunity to recognize potentially problematic constructions and verbalize correct modifications. The dynamism of authentic conversations reduces opportunities for both, especially at beginning and intermediate levels.

Imagine the following scenario: A college student participates in a month-long summer course in Russia after having completed two semesters of the language. During a class break, he waits in a long line under the hot Moscow sun to buy a cold refreshment. He notices the crabby attendant makes little eye contact, unceremoniously takes orders, collects the money, and moves on to the next customer. If the student pauses to ponder his grammatical accuracy or self-correct, he will be ignored or evoke the anger of everyone present.

In this situation, the student also understands few grammar rules, which may also require significant cognitive effort to retrieve. Even such a seemingly simple interaction necessitates understanding and remembering myriad rules, ranging from simple to complex, in addition to ensuring they are being used in contextually appropriate ways. Explicit instruction imparts many, but only a fraction, of the total contained in a language (Krashen, 1982).

Learners must also attend to grammatical forms. In a controlled classroom setting with respectful peers, maintaining attention on forms may present few challenges. In real-life situations, however, while not impossible, it becomes difficult when other cognitive tasks (e.g., the content of one's message) require attention (Krashen, 1982). In addition, distractions and their emotional state pull attentional resources away from editing morphology and syntax.

An intermediate-level college student ordering lunch in Las Ramblas, a popular tourist destination in Barcelona, may feel overwhelmed and mentally scattered because of the large crowds, high noise level, and fatigue caused by jet lag. Comprehending menu options, determining the specific items to request, and understanding the waitress in a crowded room will make monitoring quite strenuous. For several weeks or months, she might end her day with headaches and wonder if Catalonia is making her sick! As she acquires more Spanish, learned language will become less necessary and monitoring less stressful.

Avoiding the Extremes

Nevertheless, advanced students shouldn't get too comfortable. Learners at all levels can exhibit extreme use of the monitor in any given situation, one of which is *overmonitoring*. Learners who overmonitor fixate on accuracy, "speak hesitantly, often self-correct in the middle of utterances, and are so concerned with correctness that they cannot speak with any real fluency" (Krashen, 1982, p. 19). They may avoid conversations or annoy interlocutors with halting speech. In study abroad programs, this can lead to social isolation and minimize language acquisition.

In contrast, those who *undermonitor* are capable of self-editing yet exclusively utilize acquired competence without concern for accuracy (Krashen, 1982). A French-speaker from the United States might jeopardize his career in international business due to presentations and emails with a distracting number of errors, many of which make comprehension difficult for his Parisian partners.

Learners should strive to maintain a balance between fluency and accuracy (Krashen, 1982). Sustaining conversational flow, in addition to producing intelligible and accurate information, should guide monitoring, not perfection and speed. The learner of Spanish ordering food in Barcelona should thus ignore harmless errors, like using the masculine definite article to ask for a hamburger (*el* hamburguesa) instead of the correct feminine version (*la* hamburguesa). This error may evoke a few chortles but it won't impede comprehension. If, however, she accidentally uses the singular form of the verb *to want* (*quiere*) instead of the plural *quieren* to order chicken sandwiches for two monolingual friends visiting from Iowa, one might go hungry. In this case, interrupting the flow of conversation to use the monitor is worth it. Not only will it enable everybody to eat, but it will also maintain a friendship!

A FINAL THOUGHT

In reality, monitoring is an art rather than a science: sometimes learners will *undermonitor*, and sometimes learners will *overmonitor*. Developmental stages prevent perfect language production from becoming a reality. Errors, therefore, are inevitable and even healthy, for they represent growth in both the first and foreign language. Given the constraints of the critical period and older learners' likely limited access to Universal Grammar, foreign-language learners will never live without errors. Dismayed readers should remember that no skill is ever perfected. Even great athletes and artists have systemic weaknesses and bad days.

Broadly speaking, they should adopt a philosophy of functionality with respect to monitor use: language comprehension and production should aim at intelligibility. Varying communication demands and learner willingness to explore grammar, endure correction, and tolerate cognitive strain are other factors which guide monitor use. Regular reassessment of them should occur when learners strategically plan language study and use. Strategically approaching language learning, however, goes beyond planning and includes preventing and repairing communication breakdowns and comprehending texts, among other actions.

DISCUSSION QUESTIONS

1. Which similarities and differences between first- and foreign-language acquisition are most surprising to you?
2. What developmental and transfer errors have you made?
3. Imagine telling peers about the research on correction. How do you think they would react?
4. For you, is using the monitor easier when speaking or when writing?
5. Which do you tend to do more: overmonitor or undermonitor?

RECOMMENDED READING

Meisel, J. (2006). The bilingual child. In T. Bhatia & W. Ritchie (Eds.), *The handbook of bilingualism* (pp. 90–113). Malden, MA: Blackwell.

Jürgen Meisel explores the development of bilingual children, a topic largely unexplored in the current chapter. He demonstrates that the rate and route of their acquisition of grammar and vocabulary are similar to, yet distinct from, those of monolingual first- and foreign-language learners.

REFERENCES

Alex, B. (2018, December 7). How did human language evolve? Scientists still don't know. *Discover*. Retrieved from http://blogs.discovermagazine.com/crux/2018/12/07/where-does-language-come-from/#.XR0oBNJ8CUk

Balter, M. (2015, January 13). Human language may have evolved to help our ancestors make tools. *Science*. Retrieved from https://www.sciencemag.org/news/2015/01/human-language-may-have-evolved-help-our-ancestors-make-tools

Chomsky, N. (1959). Review of the book *Verbal behavior*, by B. F. Skinner. *Language, 35*, 26–58. doi: 10.2307/411334

Cook, V. (1985). Chomsky's Universal Grammar and second language learning. Retrieved from http://www.viviancook.uk/Writings/Papers/AL85.htm

Corder, S. (1981). *Error analysis and interlanguage*. Oxford: Oxford University Press.

Dabrowska, E. (2015). What exactly is Universal Grammar, and has anyone seen it? *Frontiers in Psychology, 6*, 1–17. doi:10.3389/fpsyg.2015.00852

Dulay, H., & Burt, M. (1974). Errors and strategies in child second language acquisition. *TESOL Quarterly, 8*, 129–136. doi: 10.2307/3585536

Fromkin, V., Rodman, R., & Hyams, N. (2011). *An introduction to language* (9th ed.). Boston, MA: Cengage Learning.

Hauser, M., Chomsky, N., & Fitch, W. (2002). The faculty of language: What is it, who has it, and how did it evolve? *Science, 298*, 1569–1579. doi: 10.1126/science.298.5598.1569

Hauser, M., & Fitch, W. (2003). What are the uniquely human components of the language faculty? In M. Christiansen & S. Kirby (Eds.), *Language evolution* (pp. 158–191). New York: Oxford University Press.

Jackendoff, R. (1999). Possible stages in the evolution of the language capacity. *Trends in Cognitive Science, 3*, 272–279. doi: 10.1016/S1364-6613(99)01333-9

Jackendoff, R. (2006). How did language begin? *Linguistic Society of America*. Retrieved from https://www.linguisticsociety.org/sites/default/files/LanguageBegin.pdf

Krashen, S. (1981). *Second language acquisition and second language learning*. Oxford: Pergamon Press. Retrieved from http://www.sdkrashen.com/content/books/sl_acquisition_and_learning.pdf

Krashen, S. (1982). *Principles and practice in second language acquisition*. Oxford: Pergamon Press. Retrieved from http://www.sdkrashen.com/content/books/principles_and_practice.pdf

Krashen, S. (2012, November 14). *Stephen Krashen on second language acquisition at Pagoda Academy in Busan part 1* [Video file]. Retrieved from https://www.youtube.com/watch?v=shgRN32ubag

Krashen, S. (2018a). Down with forced speech. In Y. N. Leung, J. Katchen, S. Y. Hwang, & Y. Chen (Eds.), *Reconceptualizing English language teaching and learning in the 21st century* (pp. 99–106). Taipei, Taiwan: Crane Publishing Company. Retrieved from http://www.sdkrashen.com/content/articles/down_with_forced_speech_pdf.pdf

Krashen, S. (2018b). The 40 year's war. *The English Connection, 22*(3), pp. 6–7. Retrieved from http://www.sdkrashen.com/content/articles/2018_krashen_the_40_years%E2%80%99_war.pdf

Krashen, S., & Terrell, T. (1998). *The natural approach: Language acquisition in the classroom*. Hempstead, UK: Prentice Hall.

Lewis, D. (2016, June 9). Where did we come from? A primer on early human evolution. *Cosmos*. Retrieved from https://cosmosmagazine.com/palaeontology/where-did-we-come-from-a-primer-on-early-human-evolution

Lightbown, P., & Spada, N. (2013). *How languages are learned* (4th ed.). New York: Oxford University Press.

McWhorter, J. (2004). *The story of human language: Part I*. Chantilly, VA: The Teaching Company.

Ochs, E., & Schieffelin, B. (1984). Language acquisition and socialization: Three developmental stories and their implications. In R. Schweder & R. LeVine (Eds.), *Culture theory: Essays on mind, self, and emotion* (pp. 276–320). New York: Cambridge University Press.

Pinker, S. (1996, May 7). Language is a human instinct. *Edge.* Retrieved from https://www.edge.org/conversation/steven_pinker-chapter-13-language-is-a-human-instinct

Pinker, S. (2003). Language as an adaptation to the Cognitive Niche. In M. Christiansen & S. Kirby (Eds.), *Language evolution* (pp. 16–37). New York: Oxford University Press.

Pinker, S., & Bloom, P. (1990). Natural language and natural selection. *Behavioral and Brain Sciences, 13,* 707–784. doi: 10.1017/S0140525X00081061

Saey, T. (2018, August 3). The "language gene" didn't give humans a big leg up in evolution. *Science News.* Retrieved from https://www.sciencenews.org/article/language-gene-foxp2-no-humans-evolution-boost

Searle, J. (1972, June 29). Chomsky's revolution in linguistics. *The New York Review of Books.*

Skinner, B. (1957). *Verbal behavior.* New York: Appleton-Century-Crofts.

Truscott, J. (1999). What's wrong with oral grammar correction? *The Canadian Modern Language Review, 55,* 437–456. doi: 10.3138/cmlr.55.4.437

Truscott, J. (2007). The effect of error correction on learners' ability to write accurately. *Journal of Second Language Writing, 16,* 255–272. doi: 10.1016/j.jslw.2007.06.003

Van Patten, B. (2010). Some verbs are more perfect than others: Why learners have difficulty with *ser* and *estar* and what it means for instruction. *Hispania, 73,* 29–38.

White, L. (2003). *Second language acquisition and universal grammar.* Cambridge: Cambridge University Press.

Wynne, C. (2007, October 31). Aping language: A skeptical analysis of the evidence for nonhuman primate language. *eSkeptic.* Retrieved from https://www.skeptic.com/eskeptic/07-10-31/#note12

Yang, C., Crain, S., Berwick, R., Chomsky, N., & Bolhuis, J. (2017). The growth of language: Universal Grammar, experience, and principles of computation. *Neuroscience and Biobehavioral Reviews, 81,* 103–119. doi: 10.1016/j.neubiorev.2016.12.023

Yule, G. (2006). *The study of language* (3rd ed.). Cambridge: Cambridge University Press.

5

THE IMPORTANCE OF BEING STRATEGIC

By this point in the book, Augie—a hypothetical reader—would know how to generate and maintain motivation, understand the limitations and opportunities of age, and have insight into the importance of comprehension and errors. While explaining to peers the role enjoyable reading and listening materials play in fostering acquisition, he also would note the necessity of learning some grammar rules. Instead of viewing errors with the Spanish verbs *ser* and *estar*, for example, as intellectual defects, he would seek comprehensible input and also try to understand their differences—knowledge he could use when monitoring opportunities presented themselves.

Armed with this information, Augie could expect steady progress. However, it alone may not allow survival at the wedding shower hosted by his future wife's friends. Upon entering the crowded Bogotá apartment, he would feel pummeled by questions about his family, education, wedding plans, and impressions of Colombia. When both his acquired and learned systems fail to facilitate comprehension and production, he might resemble a deer in headlights. This is because he lacks *strategic competence*.

Coined by Michael Canale and Merrill Swain, the term *strategic competence* encompasses "the verbal and non-verbal communication strategies that may be called into action to compensate for breakdowns in communication due to performance variables or to insufficient competence" (Canale & Swain, 1980, p. 30). These strategies help learners "get one's meaning across successfully to communicative partners" (Dörnyei

& Thurrell, 1991, p. 17) and understand their responses. Communication breakdowns also occur in the first language and can be ignited by unfamiliarity with a topic or vocabulary.

Most people have experienced a social situation in which they nodded along as their interlocutors detailed their passion for a certain movie or literary work, yet had no clue what they were talking about. In other cases, a person's volume has made comprehension difficult, but requesting modifications would have caused embarrassment to one or both parties. Surviving—not comprehension—was the goal. One episode of the 1990s sitcom *Seinfeld* exemplifies this. Jerry Seinfeld meets his friend Kramer's girlfriend, a "low-talker." To avoid awkwardness, he responds to her with nods and verbal affirmations (David & Cherones, 1993).

Amid the noise of music, chattering friends, and screaming children, one of Augie's fiancé's friends engages him in a conversation about something related to marriage. The volume drowns out much of her speech, which also happens to contain several unfamiliar terms. Augie fears repetition and clarification will spark a conversational negotiation incapable of overcoming the noise level and his lack of vocabulary. At this point, he decides to simply *feign understanding* (Dörnyei & Scott, 1997). Nods of agreement and occasional affirmations of *sí* and *ah bueno* would encourage her to continue and eventually wrap up the conversation—hopefully.

Augie and Jerry Seinfeld both took a gamble on this strategy. The latter lost. Kramer later thanks him for agreeing to wear a ridiculous pirate-era shirt when he promotes a benefit for the poor on a national television show. Shocked at the prospect of humiliating himself in front of the entire country, Jerry initially resists but eventually acquiesces when Kramer informs him that he affirmed his girlfriend's request—even though Jerry understood nothing. The show's host ridicules Jerry by extensively discussing the shirt (David & Cherones, 1993). While Augie's conversation probably wouldn't have such a disastrous end, it could create embarrassment and surprising obligations.

A less risky alternative involves formulating a variation of what Zoltan Dörnyei and Mary Lee Scott call an *expanded response* (Dörnyei & Scott, 1997). Although Augie understands little, he realizes his fiancé's friend is focusing on children and notices her body language and rising intonation are signaling a question. He hopes to address her question by discussing a range of issues related to children: his desire for children,

children and happiness, and the challenges of raising children in the twenty-first century. While speaking, he looks for verbal and nonverbal indications of comprehension and controls the conversation by asking if she agrees or disagrees with specific statements.

WHEN UNDERSTANDING IS THE GOAL

An alternative version of the wedding shower involves Augie wanting to understand. The noise and his lack of vocabulary concern him less than his lack of comprehension. One option entails *appealing for help* (Dörnyei, 1995); in this case, he could request assistance by encouraging his interlocutor to restructure the utterance (Celce-Murcia, Dörnyei, & Thurrell, 1995). Spanish equivalents of *Could you say that another way? Can you tell me what you mean by that?* and simply *What?*—in addition to body language (e.g., frowning)—could serve as cues.

Because some body language is not universal, misinterpretations can occur. In fact, comprehension is never a guarantee; the interlocutor may also grow bored, embarrassed, or take pity on the language learner and change the topic. Prejudice against non-native speakers may cause some native speakers to become impatient and impede learner participation. In extreme cases, they might abandon the conversation.

WHEN BEING UNDERSTOOD IS THE GOAL

However, abandonment isn't always a bad thing for learners. At times, "the learner begins to talk about a concept but is unable to continue and stops in mid-utterance" (Tarone, 1981, p. 287). Augie might consider *message abandonment* if his interlocutor fails to understand him, even after several restructuring attempts. Without his interlocutor's feedback, Augie might conclude he lacks the grammar and vocabulary to express an idea and should therefore change the topic.

On the other hand, he may feel confident in his grammar and vocabulary but utilizes *pauses* and *fillers* to buy time (Celce-Murcia, Dörnyei, & Thurrell, 1995). Spanish utterances like *a ver* (let's see), *la vida es muy complicada* (life is very complicated), an elongated *pues* (well), and even *eh* (uh) give the impression of language competence, yet provide a few seconds to formulate ideas, retrieve vocabulary, and employ the monitor to construct grammatical utterances. Learners should investigate how pauses and fillers manifest in their particular target language, for they are not universally identical.

Even with the aid of these devices, exact ideas, vocabulary, and constructions can fail to arise; *approximation*, or formulating an utterance similar to the desired one (Dörnyei & Thurrell, 1991), may help Augie still achieve his communicative objectives. If he wanted to express a hypothetical statement about raising a daughter (e.g., If I had a daughter, I would teach her self-defense), yet found the Spanish subjunctive too difficult, he could utilize the simple present (e.g., People with daughters should teach them self-defense). The word for *pediatrician* might not form part of his lexicon, but he would communicate the same meaning with *doctor*. Certain terms feel too particular for approximation, which he deals with by *coining vocabulary* (Celce-Murcia, Dörnyei, & Thurrell, 1995). Childless Augie is unlikely to be familiar with the Spanish term for *bassinet* and decides to call it *la bebecamita* or *the little baby bed*. Alternatively, he could *foreignize* an English word to appear Spanish. In this case, *bassinet* gets a vowel at the end and a change of stress to become *la basinetta*. Unfortunately for Augie, neither it nor *la bebecamita* comes close to any real Spanish word, but perhaps his fiancé's friend will get what he is trying to say.

Circumlocution, or "describing or exemplifying the target object or action" (Dörnyei & Thurrell, 1991, p. 18), could help Augie avoid the erroneous (and perhaps embarrassing) results of inventing and foreignizing, while effectively conveying the general meaning of irretrievable or unknown vocabulary. Instead of creating a new term or using Spanish phonological rules for *bassinet*, Augie could describe it as *that little thing babies sleep in for the first few months of life*. Within the utterance is *all-purpose vocabulary*, such as *thing* (Celce-Murcia, Dörnyei, & Thurrell, 1995). This word alone can fill in for just about any noun.

A handful of verbs (e.g., to be, to sleep, to do, to think, to believe, to eat, to walk, to read) fulfill syntactic and content requirements for most utterances. *Good* and *bad* can function as universal positive and negative descriptors. While all-purpose vocabulary and circumlocution won't remove frustration about gaps in the target language or memory failures, they will probably produce something comprehensible to his fiancé's friend. As a bonus, she might also supply him with the correct term: in this case, *el moisés*.

As a final option, he could ask his fiancé to interpret for him (Dörnyei, 1995). By using this strategy, however, Augie forgoes not only basic speaking practice but also the development of negotiation skills and the comprehensible input which may result from both. Moreover, the feasibility of this strategy rests upon the presence of a more proficient bilingual individual who is willing to offer her services. After considering these drawbacks, he may still deem his message important, conclude he is incapable of transmitting it, and decide that seeking his fiancé's help is his best option.

Luckily for Augie, research demonstrates that he can improve his strategy use. In a study of Hungarian high school students learning English, the following strategies were targeted for instruction: topic avoidance and replacement, circumlocution, and using fillers. Slightly less than half of the participants had strategy training, while the others followed the standard curriculum or were given conversational training. Topic avoidance and replacement strategies were first exemplified and then practiced in the native language. The participants next received scenarios in English requiring use of this strategy (Dörnyei, 1995).

Circumlocution training centered on comparing and contrasting dictionary definitions, followed by noting the characteristics of stronger entries and elaborating on them. Fillers were introduced, categorized, and practiced in sample dialogues. Tests revealed that experimental groups produced better definitions and improved their use of fillers more than the other groups. The speech rate of the experimental group also significantly increased. No significant differences in the frequency of circumlocution were found among the groups, which Dörnyei (1995) ascribes to their infrequent use by participants.

A more recent study examined female Japanese college students' use of communication strategies in English classes. The experimental group read about specific strategies (e.g., asking for clarification, buying time), kept a strategy diary, and participated in training comprised of strategy review, rehearsal, performance, and evaluation. This group's speaking performance significantly improved, while the control group's did not. The former also produced significantly longer utterances than the latter, used more strategies, and improved the quality of their strategy use (Nakatani, 2005).

ONE SIZE DOES NOT FIT ALL

Readers should not conclude either study prescribes or proscribes specific strategies. Learners have dissimilar contexts, learning goals, academic backgrounds, language proficiency levels, and materials available to them. Language learners should consider such factors when making strategic decisions and eschew a static view of strategy use which encourages selecting a handful of strategies to use in all situations (Sheorey, 2006).

PRONUNCIATION STRATEGIES

This informed approach to strategy use applies to all types of language learning and use, including pronunciation. An investigation of the pronunciation strategies used by future English teachers at a Turkish university discovered their strategic practices were influenced by the demands of their coursework. However, the top five strategies were employed with similar numerical frequency, indicating the flexibility of advanced-language-learners' strategic repository (Akyol, 2013). Most of these could be modified for use by American language learners.

One high-frequency strategy—"I make up songs or rhymes to remember how to pronounce words" (Akyol, 2013, p. 1460)—seems unnecessarily taxing when so many songs are already available. In most large cities, Spanish-language radio stations play various genres of Latin music and tend to repeat current and former hits several times a day. If not available locally, the internet offers access to Spanish-language radio stations from North and South America. However, online offerings aren't limited to Spanish; French, Arabic, Hebrew, Chinese, and hundreds of other languages have an online music presence.

Learners fearing embarrassment can sing along while privately completing other tasks, such as showering and driving to work. Exercise offers a unique opportunity to combine *narrow listening* (see chapter 3) with extensive pronunciation practice. While biking and jogging, learners can repeatedly listen to a handful of songs and—depending on the number of people present and noise level—sing along at various volumes. This type of activity helps learners acquire stress and intonation patterns in an enjoyable and physically healthy way.

An extension of this idea involves visual media. Learners select entertaining movies, television programs, and online videos, repeatedly view them, and mimic characters' stress, intonation, and pronunciation of individual sounds. Differences based on gender, social class, region, and emotional state should become clear. In addition, facial expressions and posture often accompany speech patterns. The artificial nature of some media can obscure reality, so the slapstick of comedies like *El Chavo del Ocho* shouldn't act as a precise guide for normal linguistic behavior.

Another top strategy—"I record my own voice to hear my pronunciation" (Akyol, 2013, p. 1460)—could be utilized in an American context, yet only with a correct understanding of language learning and acquisition. If errors are viewed as intellectual deficits or signs of laziness, such an activity could quickly become an exercise in self-loathing. As chapter 2 demonstrates, the critical period imposes limits on language learners, so non-native pronunciation permanently lives in their mouths. However, if learners focus on *learning* specific pronunciation features appearing in these recordings, their monitor can later use such information to self-correct.

Chapter 2 also shows the rolled *R* in Spanish flummoxes many native speakers of English, but the sound distinguishes words like *caro* (expensive) from *carro* (car) and *pero* (but) from *perro* (dog), and therefore holds communicative significance. Learners can practice holding their tongue in the appropriate position while pronouncing the sound in individual words, phrases, or entire sentences or dialogues. These recordings need not limit themselves to sounds, but can function to remind English speakers to place stress on the penultimate syllable of specific words like *policía, panadería,* and *droguería*.

Moreover, communication and pronunciation strategies can be utilized in the same context, as suggested by one study of American college students from three different Spanish proficiency levels (Peterson, 2000). One reported strategy, *proximal articulation* (i.e., selecting a sound similar to one that is challenging to produce), could be combined with *circumlocution* to increase the interlocutor's likelihood of comprehending a difficult word like *otolaryngologist*, an equally thorny term in Spanish (*otorrinolaringólogo*). In addition to modifying his pronunciation, a learner could say, *You know, the type of doctor who examines your ears, nose, and throat.*

LISTENING STRATEGIES

The successful use of listening strategies (e.g., determining what to listen to and what to ignore; using background knowledge to understand oral texts) is often a prerequisite to executing both communication and pronunciation strategies. Utilizing songs for pronunciation practice entails determining which information merits attention and which should be ignored. To comprehend his fiancé's friend, Augie could make use of his knowledge about her, his fiancé, Colombia, and marriage to construct meaning.

Not surprisingly, a review of research spanning decades found differences between more proficient listeners and less proficient listeners. The former utilize a greater variety of strategies than the latter, and their strategy use tends to be creative and focused on main ideas and text structure. Compared to less proficient listeners, they can concentrate better on sizeable pieces of discourse, more efficiently attend to the text, more consistently monitor their comprehension, employ more content and linguistic knowledge to understand what they hear, and guess the meaning of a greater volume of lexical items (Berne, 2004).

Less proficient listeners concentrate on individual words instead of main ideas, frequently translate into their first language, easily lose focus, fixate on pronunciation, and avoid inferring meaning from context. They also rarely confirm beliefs about the topic at hand and seldom employ content and linguistic knowledge to understand what they hear. In short, these listeners focus on local rather than global elements, seem to lack purpose, and use few resources when listening (Berne, 2004).

In one study, Chinese college students learning English completed a listening strategy questionnaire after a class which consisted of listening to English-language programs, taking notes, and filling in parts omitted from written transcripts. This was followed by a listening proficiency test. The results showed listening strategy use explained 22 percent of the test score variance. Scores positively and significantly correlated with strategies which directed listeners' attention, involved knowledge of their abilities, and required problem solving. Scores negatively and significantly correlated with mental translation strategies (Goh & Hu, 2013).

Research has also found connections between listening strategies and motivation. Middle school–aged learners of Canadian French filled out a listening strategy questionnaire, completed a motivation survey, and took a listening proficiency test. The results revealed a negative and significant correlation between listening proficiency and amotivation. Amotivation positively and significantly correlated with abandoning hard listening tasks. It negatively and significantly correlated with six strategies, the strongest of which was "When I have trouble understanding, I keep on listening because I expect to understand more later" (Vandergrift, 2005, p. 80).

However, extrinsic motivation (see chapter 1) positively and significantly correlated with six individual strategies, while intrinsic motivation (see chapter 1) positively and significantly correlated with ten individual strategies. Several strategies positively and significantly correlated with both types of motivation, including "When I am having trouble understanding, I tell myself that I'll manage and do fine," "When I have trouble understanding, I pay more attention and focus harder," and "When my mind wanders, I usually recover my concentration right away" (Vandergrift, 2005, p. 80).

The late linguist Larry Vandergrift put forth two reasons why listening strategies merit a disproportionate amount of practice and instruction: (1) More time is consumed listening than speaking, and (2) comprehension is the principal source of production. Moreover, simultaneously learning to comprehend and speak without strategies for coping with massive amounts of language, which "short-term memory (STM) is not capable of retaining" (Vandergrift, 1999, p. 169), can cause cognitive overload.

He recommends learners first develop *metastrategic awareness*; in short, they need to know that strategies cultivate comprehension and be equipped to use them. Several practices designed for teachers can be adapted for individual use. Learners can listen to recorded language, identify cues that suggest the text's meaning, and speculate why they do so. This fosters awareness of strategies, in general, and exposes them to instances of specific strategies. Learners should also plan to listen. Before listening to songs and podcasts and watching TV programs and movies, they should note the things they know about them and formulate a purpose. This knowledge can help generate content predictions (Vandergrift, 1999).

While listening, learners should monitor their comprehension, which consists of comparing their predictions to what they are hearing, in addition to determining the efficacy of specific strategies and making changes, if necessary. Vandergrift (1999) claims comprehension monitoring can be improved by using transcripts of spoken texts and having another person remove individual vocabulary and chunks of the texts. With the remaining product, learners can infer meaning from context and guess the missing text. Ideally, this would be done in pairs or groups, which would permit learners to explain their rationale for specific conclusions.

Finally, learners can use the *Metacognitive Awareness Listening Questionnaire (MALQ)*. The instrument consists of five strategy types: problem-solving (e.g., utilizing background knowledge to decipher unknown vocabulary); planning and evaluation (e.g., establishing a listening goal); mental translation (e.g., translating each word); person knowledge (e.g., listening in the target language is more challenging than reading, writing, and speaking for some learners; other learners feel they gain more from visuals than listening); and directed attention (e.g., getting back on track after losing concentration) (Vandergrift, Goh, Mareschal, & Tafaghodtari, 2006).

Learners can fill out the instrument to discover their strategy use and question their level of understanding, in addition to the appropriateness with which they utilize individual strategies. Occasionally, they can repeat the exercise and compare their strategy use during certain periods. Doing so may potentially "positively influence students' attitudes and their perceptions of the listening process so that, ultimately, they can become skilled listeners who self-regulate metacognitive comprehension processes automatically" (Vandergrift, Goh, Mareschal, & Tafaghodtari, 2006, p. 452).

READING STRATEGIES

Learners can also use questionnaires to improve their use of reading strategies. One widely used tool is the *Survey of Reading Strategies* (SORS) (Mokhtari, Sheorey, & Reichard, 2008). The SORS collects data pertaining to the metacognitive strategies non-native speakers of English enact while reading, but it can be used with any target language. In the context of reading strategies, *metacognitive* concerns "knowledge of the readers' cognition about reading and the self-control mechanisms they exercise when monitoring and regulating text comprehension" (Mokhtari & Reichard, 2002, p. 249).

Three strategy categories make up the instrument: global, problem-solving, and support. Global strategies entail the acts learners engage in to regulate their comprehension, examples of which are deciding what to read and previewing. Problem-solving strategies comprise the measures employed to overcome comprehension difficulties when analyzing text (e.g., re-reading, guessing unknown words). Support strategies involve acts readers carry out to assist comprehension. Reading difficult texts aloud and paraphrasing are among examples of this strategy (Mokhtari, Sheorey, & Reichard, 2008).

As with the MALQ, learners can periodically fill out the SORS, compare previous responses, and consider the reasons for similarities and differences. Before reading specific texts, learners can review the list of strategies and predict ones they will use. Prior to reading Miguel Cervantes's seventeenth-century classic novel *Don Quixote*, for example, learners would rightfully assume re-reading, using background knowledge, and adjusting reading speed depending on text difficulty would form part of their strategic repertoire. A brief internet publication about soccer, in contrast, would probably require little more than skimming and scanning.

After completing texts, they can note whether such strategies were used and consider the reasons behind their decisions. In addition, after reading any text, learners can fill out the survey, examine the number and type of strategies they used, and draw conclusions about the demands of the text and their reading level. Comparing the strategies used with similar types of texts might reveal trends which are helpful or detrimental. For example, frequent dictionary use with classic literature may be associated with improving comprehension; alternatively, if comprehension is low and dictionary use prolongs reading time, the utility of this strategy should be rethought.

As with other skills, specific strategies cannot be universally prescribed or proscribed. However, more proficient learners strategically approach texts differently than less proficient learners. The former habitually apply a variety of strategies with higher frequency, while the latter sometimes fall back on the same strategies, regardless of their efficacy. Whereas the former tend to monitor their own comprehension and possess awareness of their lack of understanding, the latter infrequently monitor their grasp of a text and "seem not to realize they do not understand" (Mokhtari, Sheorey, & Reichard, 2008, p. 45).

Research with language learners from various first languages demon-strates the universality of such differences. One study investigated the strategy use of Chinese high school students at beginning, intermediate, and advanced levels of English. All completed the SORS. The results showed the advanced group used significantly more strategies overall and on two of the three subscales (global and problem-solving) (Zhang & Wu, 2009). A different SORS-based study with Lebanese teenagers learning English found positive and significant relationships between problem-solving strategies and reading comprehension (Ghaith & El-Sanyoura, 2019).

Not all reading strategy research exclusively relies on questionnaires. Linguist Lía Kamhi-Stein investigated the strategies used by native speakers of Spanish in their first year at a large American university. Standardized test scores indicated they possessed below-average reading proficiency in English. Kamhi-Stein had the participants engage in think-alouds, which consisted of "asking students to read silently or out loud, as they usually did, and to say everything that they were thinking when they read" (Kamhi-Stein, 1998, p. 612) in either English or Spanish.

A red circle located at the end of individual sentences reminded partic-ipants to pause and vocalize their thoughts. They practiced thinking aloud a few times before they were tape-recorded for the study. In conjunction with reading tasks and a questionnaire, the think-alouds revealed partici-pants viewed all texts as having equal importance, fixated on individual words, and relied on a limited number of strategies (e.g., paraphrasing, noting difficulties understanding text) (Kamhi-Stein, 1998).

However, think-alouds need not be limited to research projects; learn-ers themselves can engage in think-alouds to improve their strategy use. By analyzing their vocalized thoughts while reading, they "gain insights into the complexities of reading, and hence expand their understanding of what it means to be a good reader" (Farr, 2005, as cited in Mokhtari & Sheorey, 2008, p. 224). Recordings can also shed light on the appropri-ateness of specific strategies. They could demonstrate, for example, that the failure of dictionaries to aid comprehension when reading Don Quixote rests with learners' inability or unwillingness to contextualize definitions.

VOCABULARY STRATEGIES

Using dictionaries to discover the meanings of unknown words is also a vocabulary-learning strategy. Readers undoubtedly recall being told to "look it up in the dictionary" when as children they asked adults to define words. Because of these repeated directives during childhood to utilize reference materials, they may not question their value. However, scholars have long worried that dictionaries artificially prolong reading time (Pritchard, 2008), which may also cause learners to lose track of the text's overall idea. Thumbing through a dictionary several times while reading a single page can likewise trigger boredom and frustration with the lack of comprehension.

Equally as problematic is picking an incorrect definition (Pritchard, 2008). Even in their first language, few learned how to select a correct definition among the many often available, thereby casting doubt on their ability to do it in another language. Moreover, beginning- and even intermediate-level learners may struggle to comprehend dictionary entries, which could cause further confusion and frustration. Finally, learners may not contextualize definitions, leading to inaccurate understandings of vocabulary.

Efforts to contextualize words may reduce erroneous interpretations. If a term contains several definitions, learners should ask themselves the following questions: *What is the most likely definition? What factors in the sentence and in the text, as a whole, lead me to that conclusion?* After selecting a definition, learners could then find a synonym, use it in that sentence, and check for intelligibility. Electronic dictionaries and glosses may reduce the time required to look up terms and thereby lessen the possibility of losing focus (Hulstijn, Hollander, & Greidanus, 1996).

If the meaning still remains unclear, learners could type the word into a search engine and examine how various websites contextualize it. But before using a paper dictionary or electronic resource, learners first need to determine whether to look up a term. If it is key to overall textual understanding or "the reading comprehension task could not be accomplished without knowing the meaning" of it (Peters, 2007, p. 36), then learners should consider looking it up. If a Spanish-speaking learner of English were asked to evaluate the fairness of a court case involving *larceny*, knowing that term would help her establish the magnitude of the crime and resulting punishment.

While certain words may be unfamiliar to learners and seemingly disassociated from key ideas and supporting points, their high frequency within a text suggests their importance. However, decisions about dictionary use should also consider reading purpose. When reading for pleasure, learners need only concern themselves with getting the overall idea. If the objective is academic and includes vocabulary assessment, dictionary use may become more of a reality (Pritchard, 2008).

Learning vocabulary independently from listening and reading contexts is possible, yet it is only advisable for specific purposes, such as formal testing. Memorization, a technique associated with word learning, has not been associated with successful language learning (Gu & Johnson, 1996), perhaps because it fosters great boredom. Other methods, such as repetition, might provide short-term value, especially when done aloud (Gu, 2003), yet will also probably lead to boredom.

A FINAL THOUGHT

Understanding and using strategies might seem like a lot of work. While this may be true, readers should remember that strategic knowledge is developed over a long period and is not a one-and-done event. Moreover, as proficiency in the target language and strategic knowledge grow, many strategies become automatic, so learners lack awareness of their use.

Those already overwhelmed or bored with strategies will be relieved to know that successfully understanding language and effectively using it require something less technical and usually of high interest to learners: cultural awareness. This often involves discovering cultural differences that seem cool. However, these differences find their way into grammar, vocabulary, and other aspects of language—and, as the next chapter demonstrates, they can challenge learners' values and perceptions of the world.

DISCUSSION QUESTIONS

1. What is one strategy you didn't know about before reading this chapter? How will you use it?

2. In your experience, are *communication strategies* facilitated more by extrinsic or intrinsic motivation? Explain.
3. Identify a strategy you used prior to reading this book. Has this chapter changed your mind about how and when to use it? Explain.
4. Name a specific strategic you tend to avoid. Explain why you avoid it.
5. How have you changed your mind about strategy use, in general, after reading this chapter?

RECOMMENDED READING

Khaldieh, S. (2000). Learning strategies and writing processes of proficient vs. less proficient learners of Arabic. *Foreign Language Annals, 33,*
522–533. doi: 10.1111/j.1944-9720.2000.tb01996.x

This article focuses on an area unexamined in the current chapter: writing strategies. Specifically, it details the strategies of American college students when writing in Arabic. Moreover, it explains and exemplifies writing strategies learners can use in any language.

REFERENCES

Akyol, T. (2013). A study on identifying pronunciation learning strategies of Turkish EFL learners. *Procedia-Social and Behavioral Sciences, 70,* 1456–1462. doi: 10.1016/j.sbspro.2013.01.211

Berne, J. (2004). Listening comprehension strategies: A review of the literature. *Foreign Language Annals, 37,* 521–533. doi: 10.1111/j.1944-9720.2004.tb02419.x

Canale, M., & Swain, M. (1980). Theoretical bases of communicative approaches to second language teaching and testing. *Applied Linguistics, 1,* 1–47. doi: 10.1093/applin/I.1.1

Celce-Murcia, M., Dörnyei, Z., & Thurrell, S. (1995). Communicative competence: A pedagogically motivated model with content specifications. *Issues in Applied Linguistics, 6*(2), 5–35.

David, L. (Writer), & Cherones, T. (Director). (1993). The puffy shirt. In L. Charles (Producer), *Seinfeld.* Los Angeles, CA: National Broadcasting Company (NBC).

Dörnyei, Z. (1995). On the teachability of communication strategies. *TESOL Quarterly, 29,* 56–85. doi: 10.2307/3587805

Dörnyei, Z., & Scott, M. (1997). Communication strategies in a second language: Definitions and taxonomies. *Language Learning, 47,* 173–210. doi: 10.1111/0023-8333.51997005

Dörnyei, Z., & Thurrell, S. (1991). Strategic competence and how to teach it. *ELT Journal, 45,* 16–23. doi: 10.1093/elt/45.1.16

Ghaith, G., & El-Sanyoura, H. (2019). Reading comprehension: The mediating role of metacognitive strategies. *Reading in a Foreign Language, 31*(1), 19–43.

Goh, C., & Hu, G. (2013). Exploring the relationship between metacognitive awareness and listening performance with questionnaire data. *Language Awareness, 23,* 255–274. doi: 10.1080/09658416.2013.769558

Gu, P. (2003). Vocabulary learning in a second language: Person, task, context and strategies. *TESL-EJ, 7,* 2. Retrieved from https://www.tesl-ej.org/wordpress/issues/volume7/ej26/ej26a4/

Gu, Y., & Johnson, R. (1996). Vocabulary learning strategies and language learning outcomes. *Language Learning, 46,* 643–679. doi: 10.1111/j.1467-1770.1996.tb01355.x|

Hulstijn, J., Hollander, M., & Greidanus, T. (1996). Incidental vocabulary learning by advanced foreign language students: The influence of marginal glosses, dictionary use, and reoccurrence of unknown words. *The Modern Language Journal, 80,* 327–339. doi: 10.2307/329439

Kamhi-Stein, L. (1998). Profiles of underprepared second-language readers. *Journal of Adolescent & Adult Literacy, 41,* 610–619.

Mokhtari, K., & Reichard, C. (2002). Assessing students' metacognitive awareness of reading strategies. *Journal of Educational Psychology, 94,* 249–259. doi: 10.1037//0022-0663.94.2.249

Mokhtari, K., & Sheorey, R. (2008). Summary, applications, and future directions. In K. Mokhtari & R. Sheorey (Eds.), *Reading strategies of first and second language learners: See how they read* (pp. 215–228). Norwood, MA: Christopher-Gordon.

Mokhtari, K., Sheorey, R., & Reichard, C. (2008). Measuring the reading strategies of first- and second-language readers. In K. Mokhtari & R. Sheorey (Eds.), *Reading strategies of first and second language learners: See how they read* (pp. 43–65). Norwood, MA: Christopher-Gordon.

Nakatani, Y. (2005). The effects of awareness-raising training on oral communication strategy use. *The Modern Language Journal, 89,* 76–91. doi: 10.1111/j.0026-7902.2005.00266.x

Peters, E. (2007). Manipulating L2 learners' online dictionary use and its effect on L2 word retention. *Language Learning and Technology, 11*(2), 36–58.

Peterson, S. (2000). *Pronunciation learning strategies: A first look* (Report No: ED450599). ERIC Clearinghouse on Languages and Linguistics. Retrieved from https://eric.ed.gov/?id=ED450599

Pritchard, C. (2008). Evaluating L2 readers' vocabulary strategies and dictionary use. *Reading in a Foreign Language, 20*(2), 216–231.

Sheorey, R. (2006). *Learning and teaching English in India.* Thousand Oaks, CA: Sage Publications.

Tarone, E. (1981). Some thoughts on the notion of communication strategy. *TESOL Quarterly, 15,* 285–295. doi: 10.2307/3586754

Vandergrift, L. (1999). Facilitating second language listening comprehension: Acquiring successful strategies. *ELT Journal, 53,* 168–176. doi: 10.1093/elt/53.3.168

Vandergrift, L. (2005). Relationships among motivation orientations, metacognitive awareness and proficiency in L2 listening. *Applied Linguistics, 26,* 70–89. doi:10.1093/applin/amh039

Vandergrift, L., Goh, C., Mareschal, C., & Tafaghodtari, M. (2006). The metacognitive awareness listening questionnaire: Development and validation. *Language Learning, 56,* 431–462. doi: 10.1111/j.1467-9922.2006.00373.x

Zhang, L., & Wu, A. (2009). Chinese senior high school EFL students' metacognitive awareness and reading-strategy use. *Reading in a Foreign Language, 21,* (1), 37–59.

6

CULTURAL AWARENESS: FEELINGS, WORDS, AND BODIES

As discussed in the first and second chapters, American language learners differ in many ways from their European peers, one of which concerns motivation. For the latter, learning English may take place with little motivation to explore various English-speaking cultures. Indeed, English is the international lingua franca, and thus a Swede may find himself using English while doing business in Indonesia, vacationing in Argentina, and communicating with a love interest from Kazakhstan. Encounters with native speakers of English could be infrequent, and motivation to visit the United States or Great Britain might not even exist.

In contrast, most serious American language learners demonstrate fascination with some aspect of the target language's culture. In today's world, Japanese anime, German cars, Brazilian Jiu Jitsu, and French cuisine often occupy the minds of many would-be bilinguals. The majority would also probably assign high worth to "viewpoints that differ from their own ethnic, national, or religious perspectives" (Douglas & Jones-Rikkers, 2001, p. 58). In short, they find other cultures interesting and believe valuing them is important. Such learners surely look forward to studying abroad to deepen both their cultural and linguistic knowledge.

THE CHALLENGING

Merely claiming to value other viewpoints is easy, and embracing ideas and customs that are attractive or differ little from one's own requires little effort. However, an inevitable part of language learning for monolingual speakers of English—especially during study abroad—involves encountering aspects of the culture that are unpleasant, at least from the learner's perspective. These aren't universal human maladies (i.e., violence, poverty), nor do they reflect unethical or immoral intentions on the part of the learner or speakers of the target language. However, they can challenge the learner's worldview.

Religious practice is one area that can generate feelings of unease. Governmental estimates have put religious affiliation in the United States at 78 percent (Bullivant, 2018). In states with large numbers of evangelical Christians, faith plays a particularly strong role in community life. Discussions of biblical verses freely take place in public, participation in organized worship is common, and much of the population attends religious services at least once a week; in Tennessee and Alabama, majorities do (Pew Research Center, 2014).

In contrast, monthly church attendance among self-identified Christians is low in Western Europe (22 percent). Nearly half of Norwegians (43 percent) and Dutch (48 percent) have no religious affiliation (Pew Research Center, 2018). This seemingly indifferent attitude toward religion can shock Americans raised in strong religious cultures. The 2014 Finnish documentary *The Norden* presents a dramatic example of this. It shows the anxiety experienced by Georgia-based pastor Marty McLain as he travels across Denmark and realizes the average adult has little interest in religion and few profess faith in God (Stark, 2014).

Challenges also can occur when immersed in a culture with a different faith. Religious studies professor Calvin Mercer of East Carolina University reports that students who believe only those who accept Jesus go to heaven sometimes undergo crises when making non-Christian friends. On a study abroad trip to Egypt, a simple meal at a Muslim student's home triggered profoundly distressing theological questions for one young man: "It was wonderful, but it was hard for me to enjoy it. How could these people, this family that is in many ways like mine, all go to hell? How could God send them to hell?" (Mercer, 2015, p. 81).

An easy solution to such problems would entail abandoning the target culture. However, this would fail to resolve difficult questions and would likely eliminate engagement with its language. While there is no simple and satisfying response to these issues, learners can cope with them by seeking input from those with similar experiences. For students specifically dealing with issues of faith, Mercer (2015) recommends reading the works of former missionaries, in addition to talking with like-minded peers.

While not spiritually threatening, food changes can feel extremely disruptive. Unfamiliar flavors and ingredients, in addition to different levels of sugar and spice and dissimilar portion sizes, can provoke anxiety among learners and native speakers of the target language (Knight & Schmidt-Rinehart, 2002). An investigation of college-aged Americans' adjustment during study abroad programs in Mexico and Spain found that food was one of the most challenging issues for students and their host families (Schmidt-Rinehart & Knight, 2004).

Mealtime customs also create difficulties. The use of hands to eat, chewing with one's mouth open, slurping, and talking during a meal are not viewed uniformly across cultures. The order and manner in which individuals are served and eat, the symbolic value of leaving food unfinished, perceptions of wasting food, and the speed with which one consumes a meal can be confusing for outsiders (DuFon, 2006; Furdyk, 2016; Kinginger, 2008; Praetzel, Curcio, & DiLorenzo, 1996). Even washing hands before eating can get tricky, with some cultures frowning upon alcohol-based hand rubs (World Health Organization, 2009).

It is therefore hardly surprising that Americans abroad often avoid eating local foods and instead "insist on searching out the nearest McDonald's or Starbucks" (Chin, 2013, para. 5), as Curtis Chin, the former US ambassador to the Asian Development Bank, has frequently observed. This reluctance of many Americans to *acculturate*, or modify their actions when entering an unfamiliar society (Berry, 1997) can cause unintended offense and restrict social interaction with native speakers of the target language, thereby reducing linguistic growth.

An investigation of American college students' social interaction patterns while studying abroad in France reveals how rejection of a culture's food results in missed chances for language learning. The participants felt the university's cafeteria was confusing, refused to try unfamiliar cuisine, and "found it easier to substitute a Coke or an extra cookie for a salad"

(Levin, 2001, cited in Kinginger, 2008, p. 8). Many discontinued any use of the cafeteria and opted for self-checkout lines to buy American foods at local grocery stores "in near total anonymity, without interaction in French" (p. 8).

Adjusting one's palate may be challenging, but experience has shown it can be done through changing habits and thinking rationally about food. Notions of food are rooted in experience: people eat certain foods at certain times and in certain ways (Cervellon & Dubé, 2005). Like many natives of Bogotá, Colombia, the author's wife grew up eating beef and potato soup for weekday breakfasts. For various reasons, she has abandoned this practice and now consumes a typical American breakfast: a bowl of cereal. Most other immigrants have done the same. If millions of people permanently change their eating habits, why can't Americans do so for a few weeks or months?

Americans with an aversion to kimchi, fermented soy beans, and pickled fish should consider that negative initial reactions to American food mention excessive amounts of sugar (Mirkovic, 2016), dislike of fast foods such as hamburgers and hot dogs (Shields, 2014), blandness, and high levels of grease (Simeonova, 2015). American bread, casseroles, and biscuits and gravy are simply inedible for many immigrants and international students (Willett, 2014). Given this information, which is more likely: only my culture prepares tasty food and promotes good table manners, or culinary preferences and habits are culturally conditioned?

Of course, not all immigrants and international students adjust to all foods. The author's wife has developed a taste for peanut butter—a food she despised for many years—but she still can't swallow biscuits and gravy and most commercially made white bread. American language learners need not be any different. In fact, appreciating a culture doesn't require liking everything about it. However, one should commit to a level of openness that sometimes feels unpleasant but which ultimately leads to a richer experience and regular contact with the target language.

WORDS

Sapir-Whorf Hypothesis

A by-product of being willing to learn another language is developing an awareness of the values, customs, and beliefs that underpin it and one's native tongue (Baker, 2012). Such a statement is now a truism, as linguists have been investigating the relationship between language and culture for more than a century. Perhaps the oldest and surely the most widely discussed product to result from such inquiry is the *Sapir-Whorf hypothesis*. In short, it asserts that "language controls both thought and perception" (Hunt & Agnoli, 1991, p. 377).

Formulated during the second and third decades of the twentieth century by Yale anthropologist Edward Sapir and Benjamin Whorf, an insurance inspector with an interest in linguistics, the Sapir-Whorf hypothesis put forth the notion that languages act as filters through which their speakers see the world. Put another way, each language "is itself the shaper of ideas, the program and guide for the individual's mental activity" (Whorf, quoted in Werner, 1997, p. 77).

Research on various aspects of Native American and European languages, particularly colors, supported this notion of linguistic relativity. Supporters claimed Navajo speakers use one word for blue and green, Latin doesn't have an all-purpose gray, and Russian speakers differentiate between sky blue and dark blue. According to the hypothesis, these classifications correlate with speakers' perception of physical reality. Moreover, Eskimo possesses unique words for snow, enabling its speakers to recognize subtitles inaccessible to those without such a rich vocabulary. Finally, Whorf claimed that Hopi grammar lacked the tense and vocabulary to indicate time as experienced in Western languages (Pinker, 1994).

While the Sapir-Whorf Hypothesis may seem intuitively appealing, its foundations rest on shaky empirical ground. Not having a word for a color does not preclude recognition of it (Pinker, 1994). This applies to other realities humans experience. The Hebrew Bible, for example, contains no word for *human rights*, but the notion finds itself implied in several passages (Bland, 2014). A young child's vocabulary may lack the term *abuse*, but that child still suffers when verbally and physically abused. In 1980, the term *AIDS* had not yet been coined, yet those with the illness still experienced the miserable death it caused.

The supposed vast number of Eskimo words for snow is also doubtful. Linguist Geoffrey Pullum has gone so far as to call it a "hoax." He explains that a simple comparison of English and Eskimo morphology in a book written by famed anthropologist Franz Boas inexplicably inspired Whorf to claim the latter language contains seven words for snow. Despite linguists' efforts to eradicate the myth, it has persisted, and the number of supposed Eskimo words for snow only grows (Pullum, 1989). Besides, there are many Inuit-Yupik-Unangan languages, not one *Eskimo* language, a term now considered offensive (Alaska Native Language Archive, 2019).

Pullum (1989) explains that those living in cold climates would surely have a richer vocabulary for snow than those from a desert-based community. All individuals living in a specific climate or working in a skilled activity possess a vocabulary for it which is unknown to others. This is clear to anyone who has listened to a doctor's diagnosis or an electrician's explanation of a home wiring problem and felt nothing but confusion. These and other professionals use specific vocabulary not because their language demands it but rather because their reality demands it of their language.

Claims of the Hopi language's lack of time also have turned out to be false. There is no evidence that Whorf, in particular, had any familiarity with the language, leading psychologist Steven Pinker to conclude his claims were based more on folklore than science: "No one is really sure how Whorf came up with his outlandish claims, but his limited, badly analyzed sample of Hopi speech and his long-term leanings toward mysticism must have contributed" (Pinker, 1994, p. 63).

Finally, if language controlled thought, then translation—and, by extension, learning another language—would prove impossible (The Linguist List, n.d.), and many cultures would not exist. Democracy, for example, has its origins in the ancient Greek city-states, and early philosophical writings on it most certainly weren't composed in English. The foundational works of Judaism and Christianity utilize Hebrew and Greek, yet most adherents of these faiths have little knowledge of these languages.

Semantics

Even though language doesn't control thought, *semantics*, or "the conventional meaning conveyed by the use of words, phrases, and sentences of a language" (Yule, 2006, p. 100), can teach language learners much about the target language's history and culture. This is especially true for words and expressions which don't exist in the learner's first language. The Hebrew word *hasbara*, for example, can be loosely translated as "a positive synonym for 'propaganda'" (Schleifer, 2003, p. 123). However, its justification is entrenched in the long-term physical and spiritual survival of the Jewish people.

In the context of the modern state of Israel, it involves promoting the attractive aspects of the country (e.g., its embrace of Western values, status as a democracy, and technological developments) to gain popular, political, and economic support on an international stage. Engaging in *hasbara* is also viewed as essential for Israel to maintain moral authority, particularly concerning its various regional armed conflicts (Schleifer, 2003).

However, some sort of *hasbara* has existed for much of Jewish history. Since Greek and Roman dominance of the Holy Land, through the Middle Ages, and up to the current day, Jews have survived by demonstrating the value of their faith and ability to be good citizens. Ancient rabbis engaged in *hasbara* with Roman officials following a failed revolt to spare Jewish survivors and allow them to open religious schools. Their medieval counterparts did so to thwart forcible conversions to Christianity. After the French Revolution, secular communal leaders used *hasbara* to help Jews gain the same rights as their Christian neighbors (Schleifer, 2003).

Two Colombian words—*palanca* and *vacuna*—also reflect a people's challenging history. The former denotes *lever* in Colombian Spanish, but it entails relationships with influential individuals (Fitch, 2012). To obtain admission into a prestigious university, a young man might ask his wealthy uncle to call the head of admissions, a childhood friend. This is *palanca*. A recent college graduate is seeking work at a prestigious company. The bank headed by her aunt has given this company many loans, so she asks her to take advantage of their relationship to better the chances of gaining employment. This is *palanca*.

Palanca's importance isn't limited to the elite. In a society with high rates of unemployment and few opportunities for social mobility, making inroads into professional life largely depends on *palanca*, even in careers which lack high status and barely provide middle-class incomes (e.g., education, nursing, social services). While utilizing personal relationships for professional gain may offend the American ideal—or myth—of meritocracy advanced by the Founding Fathers, *palanca* simply reflects an unignorable reality for Colombians.

Vacuna also represents the challenging reality of Colombian society. Instead of helping advance people's lives, it saves them. In the country's decades-long civil war, revolutionary groups, paramilitary organizations, and drug cartels have utilized *vacuna*—or *vaccination* in English—to fund themselves. Individuals, families, farmers, and business owners are threatened with kidnapping, violence, and death if they fail to regularly pay these criminal organizations *vacuna* (Gutiérrez Sanín, 2004). At best, victims receive some degree of protection from competing groups.

In addition to class structures and conflicts, words can uncover norms regarding social relations, one example of which is the Japanese term *enryo*. It seems to possess elements of self-control, reluctance, and respect, yet it also involves not explicitly challenging the views of the majority or one's interlocutor and keeping one's feelings private. As a guest in a person's home, Japanese must show *enryo* by eating and drinking what is served (Wierzbicka, 1991).

Enryo's meaning becomes clearer when it conflicts with another culture's values. Takeo Doi, a psychiatrist from Japan, discovered that his sense of *enryo* made socializing stressful in the United States. During one trip, he found himself violating *enryo* by responding to questions about his predinner cocktail choice and the manner in which his hosts should prepare it. Of course, in the United States, choice is a key cultural value; thus standard American etiquette to make guests feel welcome was being followed. Little did his hosts know the most comfortable Takeo felt was when he had no choices (Wierzbicka, 1991).

Another term that illuminates Japanese culture is *giri*, a term related to duty. It can involve returning a favor, whether large or small (e.g., a loan for thousands of dollars vs. a loan for lunch money); it can have a momentary or eternal character; it may involve honoring relatives (e.g., bringing a gift to one's elderly uncle); and it sometimes instills a feeling of being encumbered. Fulfilling *giri* might entail discomfort, yet a failure of *giri* generates feelings of disappointment and hurt by the receiving party, while it bestows shame and negative judgment on the individual who fell short (Wierzbicka, 1991).

Pragmatics

Understanding a culture not only involves learning new concepts but also becoming aware of how language is used in specific contexts. Known as *pragmatics*, the appropriate use of language extends beyond individual words to encompass acts of communication, which non-native speakers frequently get wrong (Bardovi-Harlig, 2013).

A fascinating study of one twenty-nine-year-old immigrant from Mainland China, Ming, exemplifies how cultures don't necessarily address topics in the same way. Before arriving in the United States, Ming had worked in several professional positions in her native country. These impacted her professional behavior in the United States. In one instance, she approached a woman with hiring responsibilities in a local business and relayed her parents' story: Two former professors in China who found themselves with little money and were struggling to support themselves and their daughter (Li, 2000).

As a result, they felt Ming should look for employment to cover household costs. Because she made no direct request for a job, the employee couldn't immediately figure out the purpose of such an elaborate story. In another instance, Ming approached the study's author in what seemed like an opportunity to brag about the job interview she had obtained; only after several minutes into the conversation did her request for interview preparation help become evident (Li, 2000).

Chapter 4 discussed transferring grammatical patterns from the first language into the target language, which can result in erroneous constructions. Such transfer can also occur with pragmatics and is perhaps clearest with routine "staples of communicative life" (Green, 2014, para. 1), such as *requests, refusals, greetings, and leave-taking formulae.* Imagine an immigrant to the United States comes from a culture which values directness, and thus when he notices his neighbors' long grass, he nonchalantly tells them *You need to mow your lawn* as they are getting into their cars to leave for work.

While the immigrant is merely trying to remind them to mow their lawn, his words would feel harsh in the author's native Iowa. He would come across as rude, bossy, and unhelpful. A more native-like manner to approach the subject would involve noticing the neighbor grilling burgers, making a joke from across the fence about how he'd love to have dinner in a few minutes, and then crossing the fence to chitchat. After a few minutes of friendly talking, he could subtly suggest some action with a simple observation such as *Hey, I notice your grass is growing really fast this year.* Low-level embarrassment is probably the worst possible outcome in this scenario.

Refusals can also reflect first-language norms and cause unintended negative feelings if such norms diverge from those used in the target language. Turning down a party invitation, for example, inevitably causes some hurt, but it becomes significantly worse when delivered in a manner perceived as insensitive. Research suggests such miscommunication is common. One study compared the refusals used by Thai learners of English and native speakers of English and found the former used fewer expressions of gratitude (e.g., thanks for the invitation) when rejecting invitations (Wannaruk, 2008).

Greetings, on the other hand, seem more universal, and can feel simple enough, especially if individuals with a close relationship reunite after a long period of physical separation. They smile, hug (or kiss), express joy at seeing each other, and ask about the enjoyability of the trip. But this pattern is American. While in many Latin American countries, the parties will do similar things, they frequently comment on each other's physical appearance. Upon picking up the author's wife at the Bogotá airport, one of his brothers-in-law told her she had a lot of gray hair. Another brother-in-law told the author *estás gordo* (you're fat) after hugging him!

Although deeply hurtful to Americans, such frankness doesn't have the sting in countries less obsessed with body image yet with much smaller rates of obesity and weight-related ailments. However, people from these countries may find American *leave-taking formulae* hurtful. In the United States, ending a conversation is frequently carried out with a promise to call an interlocutor or meet for further socializing (e.g., *We'll have to have you at the house for dinner; I'll give you a call soon*), words rarely taken seriously (Bou Franch, 1998).

In the Iowa of the author's youth, statements like *take care, have a good weekend,* and *give your parents my best* typically ended conversations. In fact, the absence of these or similar utterances could indicate hostility or indifference. In contrast, they showed dishonesty for many international students at his Minneapolis-based college. His Swedish-born roommate would fume about their meaninglessness and reacted with confusion when informed they were merely tools to end conversations.

On the other hand, the author reacted with confusion when international students discussed *honorific registers*, or different ways of addressing individuals depending on their social status and one's relationship to them (Agha, 1998). Many of these distinctions are embedded within the language's grammar. In Spanish, for example, there are generally two registers, formal and informal, indicated by *usted* and *tú*, respectively. The verbs accompanying them utilize different suffixes. The verb *trabajar* (to work) becomes *trabaja* when formal and *trabajas* when informal. The verb *querrer* (to want) becomes *quierre* when formal and *quierres* when informal.

These examples demonstrate that verbs in the second-person singular end with vowels in the formal register and -*S*- in the informal register. While understanding the technicalities that govern both forms requires some effort, determining levels of formality within a specific community can become frustrating. In addition, not all Spanish-speaking countries approach this issue in the same way. In Spain, for example, *tú* is utilized far more than in Colombia.

It should come as no surprise that perhaps the most socially liberal Spanish-speaking country, Spain, utilizes the informal register in many situations. However, *usted* appears to still maintain normative status when speaking with an elderly person. Moreover, register is fluid in individual contexts. Two people may begin a conversation using the formal register, discover they have a common friend, and then switch to the informal register.

BODY

Haptics

Culture is manifested through words, but also with the body. Known as *nonverbal communication,* it can take many forms, one of which is *haptics,* or "permissible physical contact between speakers" (Allen, 1999, p. 473). Northern European (e.g., Germany) and East Asian (e.g., Japan) cultures touch less than Mediterranean cultures (e.g., Greece, Italy), although this varies depending on context and individuals' relationship (Remland, Jones, & Brinkman, 1991). Interestingly, haptics may be an indicator of gender roles, which differ considerably, even within Western countries.

In one study investigating levels of touch exhibited by Czech, American, and Italian males and females in their twenties, Czech males were found to attempt hand contact with females almost three times more than American males, and Italian males attempted nonhand contact (e.g., hugging, kissing) with females almost three and a half times more than American males. Czech males uniquely initiated hand contact with females significantly more than females did with them. The authors suggest such results could symptomize male control and point to the Czech Republic's comparative lack of gender-related legislation (Dibiase & Gunnoe, 2004).

While too much touch may cause discomfort for Americans, too little can do the same. In the United States, shaking hands is a sign of goodwill, while refusal represents rudeness. The millions of Asian immigrants who shake hands every day may have been raised in countries where such touch is not normative. In India and Sri Lanka, for example, individuals often "hold their hands together in a prayerlike position, nod their heads slightly, and say namaste for both greetings and farewells" (Singh, McKay, & Singh, 1998, p. 408). In Japan, bowing is a customary greeting in which status determines depth and duration (Nomura & Saeki, 2009).

Still other haptic norms may shock many Americans, especially when they involve members of the same gender showing affection. It is not unusual for Italian men, for example, to greet each other with kisses. And while in Israel more than twenty years ago, the author noted how the extensive hand-holding and arm-locking some religious men displayed while dancing would feel too intimate for most males in the United States.

Proxemics

Standing too close to another man, especially when face to face, would also make men from the author's home state feel uncomfortable. In general, Americans aren't fans of the close talker. This sentiment is encoded in the phrase *to get in my personal space*, exemplified by a *Seinfeld* episode in which Jerry and his parents feel conflicted about Elaine's boyfriend, Aaron. Although charming, respectful, and generous, Aaron looked as if he were about to kiss them during conversations (David & Cherones, 1994).

Like haptics, *proxemics*, or the space between people when sitting or standing, differs across cultures. Similar to haptics, "there are also variations based on sex, social status, environmental constraints and type of interaction" (Jan, Herrera, Martinovski, Novick, & Traum, 2007), as the *Seinfeld* episode shows. While Americans seem to guard personal space, other cultures do so even more, yet males and females differ in their need for space. Psychologists Nan Sussman and Howard Rosenfeld demonstrated this in their study of the proxemic behavior of Japanese, American, and Venezuelan university students in the United States.

Participants were partnered with a peer from the same country and gender. They were instructed to discuss their favorite sports and hobbies. Sussman and Rosenfeld (1982) observed that Japanese participants sat significantly farther apart than their American and Venezuelan counterparts. Venezuelan and American females also sat significantly closer than their male compatriots, yet there were no gender differences observed between Japanese males and females.

A more recent study examined a wider range of countries. Students from four continents participating in a summer space program in Bremen, Germany, took part in semistructured interviews in which they were instructed to sit wherever they pleased when they arrived at the study's setting. The results showed that Anglo-Saxons (i.e., individuals from Great Britain, English-speaking Canada, and the United States) sat farthest away from the interviewer, followed by Asians, Northern Europeans, and Latinos. However, females from these groups sat closer to the researcher than males (Beaulieu, 2004).

Kinesics

Kinesics, or using movement to communicate (Allen, 1999), represents a third area of body language learners should consider, especially *eye contact* or *gaze*. It might feel like a normal by-product of talking, but eye contact can represent trust, attention to an interlocutor—or lack thereof— respect, intimidation, and even sexual interest. While certain cultures generally make more eye contact than others, reducing peoples to eye contact vs. no eye contact fails to appreciate their nuances.

In Arab-speaking countries, male-to-male eye contact normally lasts longer than male-to-male eye contact in the United States. On the other hand, eye contact with members of the opposite gender outside one's immediate family is often discouraged and thus is less likely to occur than in the United States. Religious beliefs which emphasize chastity play a significant role in such patterns. In fact, individuals with high levels of religiosity might even look down upon encountering unfamiliar members of the opposite gender (Feghali, 1997).

Positioning of the eyes can differ when thinking—even when nobody else is around. One study compared the eye contact of white Canadians, Trinidadians, and Japanese university students when answering questions in front of a camera and with an interviewer. Trinidadians maintained the most direct eye contact, while Japanese maintained the least. White Canadians and Trinidadians tended to look up when pondering the interviewer's questions, but their Japanese peers faced down (McCarthy, Lee, Itakura, & Muir, 2006). In a later study focusing only on Japanese and white Canadian students, Japanese students were seen facing down when thinking, irrespective of if they were alone or with others. Canadians, on the other hand, faced down when alone, but looked up if in the company of others (McCarthy, Lee, Itakura, & Muir, 2008).

Culture also manifests itself with inanimate objects in virtual environments. Research carried out with British and Japanese males and females in their twenties investigated their eye movement while they looked at computer avatars. While British participants focused more on the avatars' eyes, Japanese participants looked at their mouths. British participants maintained eye contact, regardless of whether avatars altered their gaze, yet Japanese participants followed the avatars' eyes, leading the authors to conclude "the eye fixation of British participants reflects the cultural expectation to maintain eye contact, but the eye fixation of Japanese participants reflects the cultural norm to conform to others' behavior" (Senju et al., 2012, p. 134).

Not surprisingly, the feelings that result from eye contact and how it reflects mood vary across cultures. A study of Finnish and Japanese university students' impressions of models' eyes in various positions evoked disparate responses. Japanese participants found direct eye contact more uncomfortable than their Finnish peers. They also reported feeling more intimidated by direct eye contact and described the models as both hostile and melancholic—conclusions not made by Finnish participants (Akechi et al., 2013).

THE LANGUAGE-LEARNER'S RESPONSE

At this point, learners might feel overwhelmed by information about body language, pragmatics, semantics, and culture, in general. Memorizing it to prevent future gaffs not only takes learners away from actual language study, but probably will prepare them to deal with only a small fraction of the cultural differences they will encounter while using the target language. Besides, just like with grammar, errors in these areas are inevitable. Berating oneself and anticipating disaster will only increase anxiety about learning.

However, having a basic understanding of these issues can foster better communication with native speakers. Conversations with immigrants and international students about cultural differences, norms of politeness, and gender relations can provide a wealth of information. Moreover, books by immigrants about language learning and culture shock can foster awareness of areas which may cause communicative difficulties.

One example is *How I Learned English: 55 Accomplished Latinos Recall Lessons in Language and Life*, which documents the linguistic and cultural challenges faced by Latin American immigrants of all ages from different countries and ethnic backgrounds. In fact, the volume's editor, Tom Miller, became interested in Spanish-speaking immigrants when he noticed how they changed when speaking English: "They had different body language. The pacing was different. The cadence was different. Their facial expressions were sometimes different. English is not just a language. It's a whole presence" (Brooks, 2007, para. 11).

Simply observing how haptics, proxemics, and kinesics function in real time can also foster such awareness. While watching a television program, movie, or online video, learners can ask themselves how these areas are functioning and note variations based upon participants' social status, gender, familiarity, age, and level of formality. Patterns will definitely emerge. Newscasters might seem excessively monotone, pedestrians may appear stoical, and bus passengers could look indifferent about touching elbows during rush hour.

Comedians—especially the children of immigrants—can shed light on cultural differences. Russell Peters, Bobby Lee, and Christina Pazsitzky are the children of Indian, South Korean, and Hungarian immigrants, respectively. Many of their stand-up routines focus on the clashing communication patterns experienced in their childhood. One constant theme regards parental comments about physical appearance, intelligence, and professional choices which seem awfully frank and even cruel in an American context.

A FINAL THOUGHT

Whatever steps learners take, they should maintain an open mind: Try new foods, meet new people, and question whether their way is necessarily the only way. Temporary discomfort eventually cedes to flexibility and a greater understanding of the world. In the process, learners have tried great food, made great friends, and collected great stories to tell the folks back home. They should also periodically assess their cultural growth and the efficacy of their actions. In fact, they should evaluate all aspects of their linguistic development. The next chapter talks about how to do this.

DISCUSSION QUESTIONS

1. How do you think trying new foods can facilitate more contact with native speakers of the target language?
2. How is culture reflected in the target language you are studying?
3. What are some of its words or expressions that would be inappropriate or strange in English?
4. How should you react when something in the target language's culture offends you? What should you not do?
5. How will you obtain a greater understanding of the target language's use of body language?

RECOMMENDED READING

Pennycook, A. (1985). Actions speak louder than words: Paralanguage, communication, and education. *TESOL Quarterly, 19*, 259–282. doi: 10.2307/3586829

This classic article reviews the importance of body language in communication and provides examples of how cultures differ in their use of kinesics and proxemics. Pennycook discusses the role of body language in language learning and recommends activities to help learners better understand it.

REFERENCES

Agha, A. (1998). Stereotypes and registers of honorific language. *Language in Society, 27*, 151–193. doi: 10.1017/S0047404500019849

Akechi, H., Senju, A., Uibo, H., Kikuchi, Y., Hasegawa, T., & Hietanen, J., (2013). Attention to eye contact in the West and East: Autonomic responses and evaluative ratings. *PLOS One, 8*(3), 1–10. doi:10.1371/journal.pone.0059312

Alaska Native Language Archive. (2019, June 4). Overview of comparative Inuit-Yupik-Unangan. Retrieved from https://www.uaf.edu/anla/collections/cea/about/

Allen, L. (1999). Functions of nonverbal communication in teaching and learning a foreign language. *The French Review, 72*, 469–480.

Baker, W. (2012). From cultural awareness to intercultural awareness: Culture in ELT. *ELT Journal, 66*, 62–70. doi: 10.1093/elt/ccr017

Bardovi-Harlig, K. (2013). Developing L2 pragmatics [Supplement]. *Language Learning, 63*, 68–96. doi: 10.1111/j.1467-9922.2012.00738.x

Beaulieu, C. (2004). Intercultural study of personal space: A case study. *Journal of Applied Social Psychology, 34*, 794–805. doi: 10.1111/j.1559-1816.2004.tb02571.x

Berry, J. (1997). Immigration, acculturation, and adaptation. *Applied Psychology, 46*, 5–68. doi: 10.1111/j.1464-0597.1997.tb01087.x

Bland, K. [Duke Center for Jewish Studies]. (2014, March 6). Kalman Bland: Medieval Jewish perspectives on human rights [Video file]. Retrieved from https://www.youtube.com/watch?v=zzhDrpeKt3Y

Bou Franch, P. (1998). On pragmatic transfer. *Studies in English language and linguistics, 0*, 5–20.

Brooks, A. (2007, September 25). Essayists reflect on studies of language and life. *NPR*. Retrieved from https://www.npr.org/templates/transcript/transcript.php?storyId=14692405

Bullivant, S. (2018, July 13). Religion is still more vibrant in the U.S. than in Europe—but there are striking exceptions to the cliché. *America*. Retrieved from https://www.americamagazine.org/faith/2018/07/13/religion-still-more-vibrant-us-europe-there-are-striking-exceptions-cliché

Cervellon, M., & Dubé, L. (2005). Cultural influences in the origins of food likings and dislikes. *Food Quality and Preference, 16*, 455–460. doi:10.1016/j.foodqual.2004.09.002

Chin, C. (2013, October 17). Studying abroad can be an expensive waste of time. *The New York Times*. Retrieved from https://www.nytimes.com/roomfordebate/2013/10/17/should-more-americans-study-abroad/studying-abroad-can-be-an-expensive-waste-of-time

David, L. (Writer), & Cherones, T. (Director). (1994). The Raincoats. In L. Charles (Producer), *Seinfeld*. Los Angeles, CA: National Broadcasting Company (NBC).

Dibiase, R., & Gunnoe, J. (2004). Gender and culture differences in touch behavior. *The Journal of Social Psychology, 144*, 49–62. doi: 10.3200/SOCP.144.1.49-62

Douglas, C., & Jones-Rikkers, C. (2001). Study abroad programs and American student world-mindedness: An empirical analysis. *Journal of Teaching International Business, 13*, 55–66. doi: 10.1300/J066v13n01_04

DuFon, M. (2006). The socialization of taste during study abroad in Indonesia. In M. DuFon & E. Churchill (Eds.), *Language learners in study abroad contexts* (pp. 91–119). Clevedon, UK: Multilingual Matters.

Feghali, E. (1997). Arab cultural communication patterns. *International Journal of Intercultural Relations, 21*, 345–378. doi: 10.1016/S0147-1767(97)00005-9

Fitch, K. (2012). Two political dilemmas in Colombian interpersonal ideology. In M. Placencia & C. Garcia (Eds.), *Research on politeness in the Spanish-speaking world* (2nd ed.) (pp. 245–260). New York: Taylor & Francis.

Furdyk, B. (2016, April 18). 14 strange food customs from around the world. *Food Network*. Retrieved from https://www.foodnetwork.ca/global-eats/photos/strange-food-customs-around-the-world/#!knife_and_fork_cutting

Green, M. (2014, October 2). Speech acts. *Stanford Encyclopedia of Philosophy*. Retrieved from https://plato.stanford.edu/entries/speech-acts/

Gutiérrez Sanín, F. (2004). Criminal rebels? A discussion of civil war and criminality from the Colombian experience. *Politics & Society, 32*, 257–285. doi: 10.1177/0032329204263074

Hunt, E., & Agnoli, F. (1991). The Whorfian Hypothesis: A cognitive psychology perspective. *Psychological Review, 98*, 377–389. doi: 10.1037/0033-295X.98.3.377

Jan, D., Herrera, D., Martinovski, B., Novick, D., & Traum, D. (2007). A computational model of culture-specific conversational behavior. In C. Pelachaud et al. (Eds.), *Intelligent Virtual Agents. IVA 2007* (pp. 45–56). Berlin: Springer.

Kinginger, C. (2008). Language learning in study abroad: Case studies of Americans in France [Supplement]. *The Modern Language Journal, 92*, 1–131. https://doi.org/10.1111/j.1540-4781.2008.00821.x

Knight, S., & Schmidt-Rinehart, B. (2002). Enhancing the homestay: Study abroad from the host's family perspective. *Foreign Language Annals, 35*, 190–201. doi: 10.1111/j.1944-9720.2002.tb03154.x

Li, D. (2000). The pragmatics of making requests in the L2 workplace: A case study of language socialization. *The Canadian Modern Language Review, 57*, 58–87. doi: 10.3138/cmlr.57.1.58

The Linguist List. (n.d.). The Sapir-Whorf Hypothesis. Retrieved from https://linguistlist.org/ask-ling/sapir.cfm

McCarthy, A., Lee, K., Itakura, S., & Muir, D. (2006). Cultural display rules drive eye gaze during thinking. *Journal of Cross-Cultural Psychology, 37*, 717–722. doi: 10.1177/0022022106292079

McCarthy, A., Lee, K., Itakura, S., & Muir, D. (2008). Gaze display when thinking depends on culture and context. *Journal of Cross-Cultural Psychology, 39*, 716–729. doi: 10.1177/0022022108323807

Mercer, C. (2015). Finding freedom abroad: Working with conservative Christian students in study abroad programs. *Teaching Theology and Religion, 18*, 81–87. doi: 10.1111/teth.12266

Mirkovic, V. (2016, September 18). Why international students don't adjust well to American food. *Beyond the Oval*. Retrieved from https://medium.com/beyond-the-oval/why-international-students-dont-adjust-well-to-american-food-f115a6fdce2b

Nomura, T., & Saeki, K. (2009). Effects of polite behavior expressed by robots: A case study in Japan. Retrieved from http://rins.st.ryukoku.ac.jp/~nomura/docs/PBC_IAT09Fin.pdf

Pew Research Center. (2014). *Attendance at religious services by state*. Retrieved from https://www.pewforum.org/religious-landscape-study/compare/attendance-at-religious-services/by/state/

Pew Research Center. (2018, May 29). *Being Christian in Western Europe.* Retrieved from https://www.pewforum.org/2018/05/29/being-christian-in-western-europe/

Pinker, S. (1994). *The language instinct: How the mind creates language.* New York: W. Morrow & Company.

Praetzel, G., Curcio, J., & DiLorenzo, J. (1996). Making study abroad a reality for all students. *International Advances in Economic Research, 2,* 174–182. doi:10.1007/BF02295057

Pullum, G. (1989). The great Eskimo vocabulary hoax. *Natural Language & Linguistic Theory, 7,* 275–281.

Remland, M., Jones, T., & Brinkman, H. (1991). Proxemic and haptic behavior in three European countries. *Journal of Non-Verbal Behavior, 15,* 215–232. doi: 10.1007/BF00986923

Schleifer, R. (2003). Jewish and contemporary origins of Israeli hasbara. *Jewish Political Studies Review, 15,* 123–153.

Schmidt-Rinehart, B., & Knight, S. (2004). The homestay component of study abroad: Three perspectives. *Foreign Language Annals, 37,* 254–262. doi: 10.1111/j.1944-9720.2004.tb02198.x

Senju, A., Vernetti, A., Kikuchi, Y., Akechi, H., Hasegawa, T., & Johnson, M. (2012). Cultural background modulates how we look at other persons' gaze. *International Journal of Behavioral Development, 37,* 131–136. doi: 10.1177/0165025412465360

Shields, J. (2014, April 22). International students speak to how American food affects their weight. *The Collegian.* Retrieved from https://www.kstatecollegian.com/2014/04/22/international-students-speak-to-how-american-food-affects-their-weight/

Simeonova, A. (2015, June 15). What international students really think about American food. *Spoon University.* Retrieved from https://spoonuniversity.com/lifestyle/international-students-really-think-american-food

Singh, N., McKay, J., & Singh, A. (1998). Culture and mental health: Nonverbal communication. *Journal of Child and Family Studies, 7,* 403–409. doi.org/10.1023/A:1022946925134

Stark, J. (2014, November 10). *The Norden-religion* [Video file]. Retrieved from https://www.youtube.com/watch?v=W-kANR1vJkM

Sussman, N., & Rosenfeld, H. (1982). Influence of culture, language, and sex on conversational distance. *Journal of Personality and Social Psychology, 42,* 66–74. doi: 10.1037/0022-3514.42.1.66

Wannaruk, A. (2008). Pragmatic transfer in Thai refusals. *RELC Journal, 39,* 318–337. doi: 10.1177/0033688208096844

Werner, O. (1997). Sapir-Whorf Hypothesis. In P. Lamarque (Ed.), *Concise encyclopedia of philosophy of language* (pp. 76–83). Oxford: Oxford University Press.

Wierzbicka, A. (1991). Japanese key words and core cultural values. *Language in Society, 20,* 333–385. doi: 10.1017/S0047404500016535

Willett, M. (2014, October 15). 17 "all-American" foods that foreigners find gross. *Business Insider.* Retrieved from https://www.businessinsider.com/american-foods-foreigners-find-gross-2014-10

World Health Organization. (2009). *WHO guidelines on hand hygiene in health care.* Retrieved from https://www.ncbi.nlm.nih.gov/books/NBK144013/pdf/Bookshelf_NBK144013.pdf

Yule, G. (2006). *The study of language* (3rd ed.). Cambridge: Cambridge University Press.

7

ASSESS YOURSELF

The first thought which comes to mind upon hearing the word *assessment* is, unfortunately, *test*. In the realm of language learning, the typical test is created by teachers for a *formative* purpose—that is, "to give feedback to improve what is being assessed" (Diaz-Rico, 2008, p. 81)— or a *summative* purpose, which "provides an evaluative summary" (p. 81) of progress over a long period, usually an academic semester. In other words, it helps teachers know how well students are doing (formative) or how well they have done (summative). For students themselves, it often merely means a grade.

The test's emphasis on "the small bits and pieces of a language" (J. Brown, 1996, p. 29) also gives it a *discrete-point* flavor. Multiple-choice items which ask students to select the correct suffix for a verb, pronunciation of a letter, and gender for an article used with a masculine or feminine noun represent the types of questions learners often encounter. Pressure to quickly answer can become intense if many items are present and time is limited. Unless given in take-home format, the test must be completed during one class period—a relatively short amount of time.

While its ease of design and administration make it attractive for teachers—and for students and parents who feel grades necessarily indicate character and level of mastery—the traditional language test suffers from several related problems, the first of which concerns its *decontextualization*. Correctly answering questions about the finer points of grammar, vocabulary, and pronunciation doesn't necessarily translate to correctly using grammar, vocabulary, and pronunciation outside the testing setting.

A related problem with the traditional test is *authenticity*, or "the extent to which a test or assessment task relates to the context in which it would normally be performed in real life" (Leung & Lewkowicz, 2006, p. 214). Unfortunately, disparate structures with unusual vocabulary usage and bizarre scenarios can easily find themselves included in formal assessment. A plastic expression like *Hello, Millicent, I wanted to enquire about your availability for the next high school formal* can follow antiquated greetings (e.g., *Welcome home, madame!*) and random exclamatives such as *Wow! What a swell job!*

Finally, there is the problem of its emphasis on *metalinguistic knowledge*, which involves "speakers' ability to talk about the language" (Truscott, 1998, p. 123) rather than their ability to use it. As discussed in chapters 3, 4, and 5, learning about language can feel taxing and inefficient and is separate from acquiring it. Many non-native speakers of English who can barely carry out a basic discussion or write a coherent summary of a short essay correctly identify parts of speech American-born graduate students have never even heard of!

SELF-ASSESSMENT

Definitions and Benefits

Fortunately, the type of assessment encouraged in this chapter, *self-assessment,* attempts to avoid the unpleasantries of traditional testing. This term is exactly as it sounds: instead of teachers carrying out evaluations, learners do them. In a classroom context, some teachers may find self-assessment attractive not only because it often requires little time to direct (J. Brown & Hudson, 1998) and reduces their labor-intensive and time-consuming grading schedules but also because it helps students grow independently and become *autonomous* learners.

Self-assessment encourages learners to "take responsibility for their learning" and "provides an opportunity to self-tailor an assessment regime which can parallel a self-tailored study regime" (Gardner, 2000, p. 51). Gardner emphasizes that this practice furnishes immediate insight into the efficacy of learners' strategies and study techniques, which prompts them to make adjustments, abandon certain practices, change nothing, or reconsider goals. Awareness of linguistic development can also foster motivation.

Finally, self-assessment is often *criterion-referenced* in nature, meaning it asks learners to evaluate themselves according to specific standards (e.g., the ability to form a question in Arabic accurately in 80 percent of obligatory contexts) (Andrade & Du, 2007). This is different from *norm-referenced* assessment, which measures performance "relative to the scores of all other students who took the test" (e.g., the frequency of correct question formation in Arabic compared to peers) (J. Brown, 1996, p. 2).

Assess What?

Obviously, a prescriptive, one-size-fits-all template for carrying out self-assessment doesn't exist and would certainly be inappropriate for many learners. Assessment practices should align with specific goals. Three broad approaches to self-assessment suggested by linguist Douglas Brown, however, address critical areas of linguistic growth and can be carried out in more than one way (D. Brown, 2004).

The first area is *assessment of a specific performance*, which involves learners monitoring their comprehension or use of texts and spoken language "immediately or very soon after the performance" (D. Brown, 2004, p. 271). Subsequent to reading a Spanish-language *National Geographic* article about whales, an intermediate-level learner of Spanish may seek to identify her overall level of comprehension and the specific structures which create difficulties. Doing so could alter the techniques she uses to comprehend similar texts in the future.

The same learner could find herself taking a tour of Spain's most important art venue, the Museo del Prado, and wonder not only how much of the general idea she picked up but also if she followed the guide's use of tense shifts and art terminology. She might likewise be curious about her ability to spontaneously construct questions comprehensible to Spanish speakers in a rather noisy public venue. Self-assessment could communicate weaknesses with specific linguistic issues (e.g., pronunciation of multisyllabic words) or a lack of overall readiness for such scenarios.

Beginning-level learners can find focus by assessing basic tasks from daily life: telling time and asking for the time; introducing oneself and greeting others; comprehending a menu and ordering lunch; purchasing groceries and understanding recipes; and comprehending public transportation information, among others. Advanced learners could focus on more lexically and grammatically complex performances, such as disputing a bill, undergoing a job interview, giving a presentation about the American political system, or writing a formal email for business purposes.

In addition to a specific performance, learners can engage in *indirect assessment of general competence* (D. Brown, 2004). In contrast to the time-restricted nature of assessing a specific performance, this can comprise assessment over a period of days, weeks, months, or even an entire year. An intermediate-level student of Spanish could assess her general speaking abilities after a three-week intensive course and homestay in Mexico City to estimate the value of a year-long study abroad program. After a summer of reading Spanish translations of classic American novels, she might find measuring her vocabulary growth and increase in confidence useful in formulating fall reading plans.

Beginning-level learners should focus on categories which encompass the tasks they have carried out during a specific time frame. For speaking, criteria could emerge from general questions such as *Do people understand when I speak? How much do I understand when engaging in basic tasks? How have I grown? Do I feel more confident in my abilities?* Because self-assessment at this stage is global, concerns about specific grammatical items should not receive emphasis. As discussed throughout this book, errors are natural and abundant for beginners.

Advanced learners, on the other hand, probably have fewer global concerns, but perhaps worry about the accuracy of specific pieces of grammar. The subjunctive in Spanish, for example, is notoriously difficult (Kanwit & Geeslin, 2014) and will be a source of frequent errors for beginning and intermediate learners. Learners who gain high levels of accuracy and fluency are likely ready to acquire this form and commit fewer errors with it as they progress. However, even occasional inaccurate use of the subjunctive may cause undesirable judgments about language proficiency, leading learners to assess this and other late-acquired forms (e.g., prepositions).

A third option is *metacognitive assessment*, which involves the assessment of goals themselves (D. Brown, 2004). Periodically, learners need to evaluate whether or not they have reached these goals and the wisdom of them. The intermediate-level learner may have entered her summer abroad program with the goals of being able to speak with more accuracy and fluency, in addition to processing conversational Spanish more quickly. Having achieved those goals, what are reasonable future goals? How will she reach them? What resources will she need to attain them?

In addition to the three areas highlighted by D. Brown (2004), learners should assess their level of stick-to-itiveness regarding the process of language learning. The intermediate learner studying in Mexico pledged to do the following on a daily basis: read leisure materials in Spanish for at least twenty minutes, watch an hour of news, socially engage two native speakers, and listen to a podcast in Spanish while on the subway. Regular assessment of her ability to carry out these actions can engender feelings of accomplishment, which can motivate her to continue or even do more. Alternatively, it may demonstrate she is doing too much.

HOW DO I ASSESS MYSELF?

Checklists and Questionnaires

Learners can use a variety of techniques to carry out self-assessment, one of which is the *checklist*. In medical research, reviewers utilize checklists to hold themselves accountable for evaluating areas which could produce erroneous science and possibly injure or kill a patient (Oxman, 1994). Thankfully, the stakes in language learning are not so extreme; however, learners can use checklists to determine whether they completed the tasks to which they committed.

The intermediate learner of Spanish could make a notebook with a column containing *yes* with rows for reading, news watching, conversations with native speakers, and podcast listening. She could carry the notebook with her and check *yes* after completion of each activity. Alternatively, she could do the checklist before bed. In this way, the checklist would serve to assess specific performances. Alternatively, it could assess her long-term ability to consistently engage the language. Periodically, for example, she might look at her success from several individual checklists—or lack thereof—to help determine if activities need modification.

Checklists can also be used to avoid specific actions. The learner knows that leisure reading should consist of enjoyable materials which are not the subject of grammatical or lexical analysis. However, she has found herself gravitating to websites focusing on boring topics, re-reading to understand everything, and looking up the meaning of all unknown words. To remind herself not to avoid such practices, she could construct a checklist with *yes* and rows consisting of things she should do (e.g., *I read an enjoyable website*) and shouldn't do (e.g., *I stopped to look up the meaning of most unknown words*).

An advanced learner of Spanish could use a checklist to assess her use of the subjunctive. In a specific performance, such as staying with a friend's family for a weekend, focusing on both comprehension and production may prove appropriate. The former can involve efforts to potentially expose oneself to comprehensible input with the subjunctive (e.g., *I participated in conversations with a variety of people*) and recognize its occurrence (e.g., *I made a mental note of when the subjunctive was used by others*).

The latter may manifest as statements about frequency of use (e.g., *I used the subjunctive when optional*) and precision of execution (e.g., *I used the subjunctive correctly more than 70 percent of the time*). Both comprehension and production can be facilitated by initiating conversations with the subjunctive and following interlocutors' responses (e.g., *I started two conversations with the subjunctive and attended to the structures speakers produced in the conversation*). The same learner might also periodically assess her general ability to use the subjunctive, which would change the tense and wording of some items (e.g., *I generally use the subjunctive correctly*).

For those for whom constructing checklist statements feels cumbersome, the *can do* format developed by the National Council of State Supervisors for Languages and the American Council on the Teaching of Foreign Languages (NCSSFL-ACTFL) offers a user-friendly linguistic template adaptable "to fit the content and context of the learning and the targeted proficiency level" (ACTFL, n.d., para. 11). While ACTFL's *can do* statements form part of a larger, highly detailed, and complex examination of language-learners' proficiency, they are fairly simple to comprehend.

In addition, many don't require modification for immediate use. A statement like "I can interact at a survival level in some familiar everyday contexts" (ACTFL, 2017, p. 1) is relevant to learners of any language, whether they are engaged in classroom or independent study. Learners desiring more nuance can respond to statements using a questionnaire format with a Likert scale, which is a tool designed to capture variation in attitude or behavior (Wakita, Ueshima, & Noguchi, 2012). It could contain five levels: 1 = never, 2 = rarely, 3 = sometimes, 4 = often, 5 = always. Learners can use this format to respond to statements they have created.

If an advanced learner were assessing herself for general ability to use the Spanish subjunctive, she would not only gain insight from the number she circled but also the explanation accompanying it. After indicating a 3 (sometimes), she could write about the circumstances under which she can use the subjunctive and those which still present difficulties, as well as her feelings. She might discover the subjunctive comes easily when discussing uncontroversial matters (e.g., movies, clothing style) but that she has trouble constructing it when debating heated topics like US foreign policy or when she knows little about the topic.

Can Learners Really Assess Themselves?

At this stage, the notion that learners can assess themselves may appear "as an absurd reversal of politically correct power relationships" (D. Brown, 2004, p. 270) since they often possess only bits and pieces of the target language. Nevertheless, research has shown learners are capable of doing so. One study investigated the relationship between intermediate-level college French learners' assessment of their pronunciation abilities and experts' ratings of them. Specifically, they examined the degree to which their pronunciation was native-like (Lappin-Fortin & Rye, 2014).

The two raters, both fluent French speakers with advanced degrees in linguistics, assessed recordings of the learners reading a written text aloud. The results indicated positive and significant correlations between learners' and raters' assessment. While the authors noted that learners' and raters' assessment of certain aspects of pronunciation failed to correlate, their overall conclusion was that "there was sufficient evidence to support the usefulness of self-assessment as a general tool when teaching pronunciation" (Lappin-Fortin & Rye, 2014, p. 313).

A study of Iranian English learners found strong relationships between self-assessment and teachers' assessment of learners' oral proficiency. A group of English majors studying at an Iranian university made a recording of their own speech and assessed it using whatever standards they felt appropriate. A group of teachers established their own criteria, which were explained to participants and used to assess them. The participants then carried out a second self-assessment with these criteria. Correlations between learners' first and second assessments and teachers' assessments were positive and strong (Babaii, Taghaddomi, & Pashmforoosh, 2016).

Not surprisingly, high agreement has been found between advanced learners' self-assessment and teachers' assessment of them. Learners of German from several different first languages were recorded while reciting sets of individual words. They listened to a group of native speakers reciting the same words and compared their pronunciation to their own performance. A group of teachers judged learners' pronunciation as well. The results showed that learner-teacher agreement was very high (85 percent) (Dlaska & Krekeler, 2008).

There is evidence that even elementary-aged children can self-assess. A study of South Korean English learners in grades four and six examined the relationship between students' self-assessment and teachers' assessment of them. Two self-assessments took place: one following a speaking task and another which asked students to rate their overall abilities. The study also investigated the relationship between learners' assessments and their scores on the Cambridge Young Learners' Test, a standardized test designed to assess the four main linguistic skills (reading, writing, listening, and speaking) (Butler & Lee, 2006).

For fourth graders, on-task self-assessment moderately correlated with teachers' assessment and the standardized exam. Both correlations between overall self-assessment and teachers' assessment and correlations between self-assessment and the standardized exam were lower. However, all correlations were positive and significant. Likewise, significant correlations were seen among sixth graders. Both on-task and overall self-assessment positively and significantly correlated with teachers' assessment and the standardized exam (Butler & Lee, 2006).

Learners also perceive that engaging in self-assessment improves their oral proficiency and the manner in which they approach language learning. Intermediate-level students of French at an Australian university participated in interviews, completed questionnaires, and answered open-ended questions at various points during a twelve-week semester. The majority of participants supported continuing self-assessment the next semester (70 percent), and the perceived benefits of it included the role of feedback in facilitating motivation, generating self-awareness, directing learners' monitoring of their language use, and inspiring a sense of accountability (de Saint Léger, 2009).

Self-assessment which consists of extensive feedback can provide learners with a thick description of their approach to learning. They can in turn utilize it to determine where and how to change. This was demonstrated in a study of Taiwanese university students in a mandatory first-year English course. The participants listened to recordings of their speech, transcribed them, and carried out evaluations of their grammar, word usage, intonation, fluency, pronunciation, content knowledge, and organization. They were also asked to discuss how they could further advance their speaking skills (Huang, 2016).

Three findings emerged from student narratives. Specifically, participants detected inconsistencies in actual vs. perceived performance; speaking strategies they could use to better their oral proficiency; and features of themselves as learners that facilitate or inhibit such improvement (Huang, 2016). *Learner diaries* outside of the classroom can also generate extensive feedback. Sometimes called *learner journals*, diaries can take a variety of formats and receive differing degrees of attention from learners, yet most tend to be *introspective* in nature (Bailey & Ochsner, cited in Bailey, 1991).

Learner Diaries

Introspection (i.e., examining one's thoughts and actions) can occur simultaneously with, directly following, or even significantly after a linguistic event. Ideally, all give learners insight into phenomena invisible to others (Peirce, 1994). This was evidenced by a study of university-level English learners in Argentina. Diaries kept over thirty-five weeks revealed their attitudes toward learning, in addition to the circumstances they believed promoted learning and motivation. Notably, participants "gained consciousness of themselves as managers of their own learning and developed as individuals with personal learning purposes to be pursued at all costs" (Porto, 2007, p. 692).

In another study, a small group of Thai students in an English graduate program kept diaries in which they addressed questions about the quantity and quality of the content they learned, the strategies they used to learn, and the difficulties they encountered and how they tackled them. One participant revealed he could not remember new material unless he took notes, and thus vowed to do so more often. Another thought she comprehended class materials but discovered her lack of ability when discussing them in real time, leading her to conclude she would need to read more closely (Srimavin & Darasawang, 2004).

There is no one way to maintain a diary. In terms of frequency and length, learners should have an eye for practicality: if free time is limited to a few minutes before bed, entries may be infrequent and short (e.g., a small paragraph or two). Learners need not necessarily commit to lengthy entries, even when time is abundant. The intermediate-level learner reading a Spanish-language *National Geographic* article about whales could write a notecard-length entry discussing her level of comprehension. After completing the tour of the Museo del Prado, she could complete an entry of the same length focusing on her level of comprehension, reasons for it, and needed changes.

Entries focused on *indirect assessment of general competence* (D. Brown, 2004) probably require more time to reflect and detail experiences. The learner in the three-week program in Mexico, for example, could plan an hour once a week to assess her growth overall and on specific skills. On the last day of the program, or even on the plane ride home, she could write an even more extensive entry which included reflecting on those entries completed during the program.

The specific content addressed should align with learner goals. The learner's goals when reading the *National Geographic* article could include comprehending more than 50 percent of the article, learning five to ten new words, and completing the task in ten to fifteen minutes. Three diary questions could correspond to these goals: (1) What percentage of the article have I understood and why? (2) How many new words have I learned and what helped or prevented me from doing so? (3) How long did I need to complete the article and why?

The goals of the museum visit might consist of comprehending more than 50 percent of the tour guide's presentation and learning five to ten new words. A third goal could include focusing on global comprehension and not getting stuck on trying to comprehend individual words. The following diary questions might guide her entry: (1) How much of the presentation did I understand? What things about the tour guide, the environment, and my own proficiency level facilitated and/or inhibited comprehension? (2) What types of words did I learn? What helped me learn them? (3) Did I focus on overall meaning most of the time? Why or why not?

Weekly diary entries in Mexico would likely focus on long-term goals such as global growth (e.g., greater comprehension of spoken Spanish in informal situations); increased grammatical accuracy when speaking; and the use of more vocabulary in written and oral situations. However, assessing whether she reached these goals would require more extensive answers and examples than an assessment of a specific performance: (1) Has my comprehension of spoken Spanish improved? What evidence justifies my answer? (2) Am I using grammar more accurately than I did the previous week? If the answer is *yes*, is this because I acquired or learned more language? (3) Do I feel a growth in vocabulary? If so, what types of words, or specific words, am I using that I didn't previously know? Learners can utilize the diary macroanalysis suggested by pedagogical researcher Melina Porto to formulate conclusions: repeatedly read entries, note prominent characteristics, and look for trends (Porto, 2007).

They can also utilize her method of microanalysis, which consists of seeking "key words, revealing actions and behaviors, critical incidents, and pivotal events in the data" (Porto, 2007, p. 680). The information obtained by both types of analysis can reveal previously unnoticed progress and foster motivation, especially during periods in which learners struggle to understand others and express themselves. However, negative trends need not lead to despair.

Narrative explanations might show unrealistic goals. Expecting improved grammatical accuracy after only one week in Mexico, for example, assumes experiencing extensive interaction that will quickly translate to more precise production. Language acquisition doesn't follow such a linear trajectory. Moreover, actual social interaction with native speakers of Spanish may have been quite limited due to extensive orientation activities carried out in English, several hours of listening to Spanish-language lectures, and evening hours spent talking to worried parents. Nerves may have prevented the learner from taking advantage of speaking opportunities.

Fortunately, learners can modify goals and change the manner in which they approach them. A simple question such as *What can I do to reach these goals?* can lead them to reflect on three key areas of *metacognition*, or examination of one's own thoughts and performance: *person*, *task*, and *strategy* (Flavell, 1979). The student in Mexico may conclude she lacks patience, expects immediate comprehension, and avoids situations which may require temporary confusion and negotiation of content (*person*).

She may also discover her lack of knowledge regarding social interaction in Mexico. Approaching a classmate to get a cup of coffee in the United States is difficult enough, but she realizes she has never seen this done in Spanish (*task*). Moreover, she notes that her only way to get through a linguistically challenging conversation is by trying to understand every word, which prevents her from engaging in all but the simplest interactions (*strategy*). As a result of this reflection, she decides to make the following changes. First, she will assess grammatical accuracy upon ending the study abroad session instead of every week, thereby allowing more time for realistic growth.

Next, she will take advantage of more opportunities to speak, starting with low-risk situations such as conversations about the weather with her host mother and complimenting the school cafeteria cashier's new shoes. Meanwhile, she will prepare for more complex interactions by asking her professor to model initiating casual conversations with members of the same gender. Finally, she will seek the help of the American graduate student who speaks fluent Spanish, specifically requesting guidance on actions which repair communication breakdowns during socialization.

LIMITATIONS OF SELF-ASSESSMENT

No method of assessment is without its limitations, and self-assessment is no exception. Learners may find introspection difficult, become distracted during an activity, forget actions and thoughts, and lack awareness of everything they are doing. Unfortunately, recollections may "change with time" (Fry, 1988, p. 160), leading to checklists, questionnaires, and diaries which don't reflect reality. Designing checklists and questionnaires requires time, energy, and knowledge; writing diaries can tax one's memory; and analyzing, in addition to acting on, all of them necessitates a stable commitment to improvement.

Furthermore, learners' assessments of themselves can sometimes be plain wrong. An investigation of international students in one English-speaking Canadian university found they erroneously evaluated their own speaking abilities. Specifically, participants' self-rating showed no correlations with ratings given by native speakers of English who were also linguists. Belief in one's speaking abilities negatively correlated with native speakers' rating of accent and comprehensibility, "indicating that more accented and less comprehensible speech was associated with greater overconfidence scores" (Trofimovich, Isaacs, Kennedy, Saito, & Crowther, 2016, p. 126).

Research with target languages other than English has found similar results. Chinese learners of Japanese who had been living in Japan between three months and thirteen years completed a questionnaire which inquired about their reading skills and an objective reading exam. The results indicated that those who read in Japanese and interacted less in the language generally overrated themselves, "whereas those with more experience underestimated their skills" (Suzuki, 2015, p. 76).

Overestimation of abilities shouldn't preclude learners from utilizing self-assessment; however, it should make them vigilant—especially during the beginning stages of learning—about accurately documenting both achievements and challenges. Besides, interactions in native-speaking environments often have humbling effects on language learners, as was the case with the college-aged student who believed he was basically fluent in Russian after a twelve-week course. A study abroad trip demonstrated the contrary, and he reached advanced proficiency only after four years of intensive study (N. Brown, Dewey, & Cox, 2014).

A FINAL THOUGHT

Learners can also measure their own assessments against performance in language coursework and standardized tests, but these results should be interpreted with caution. Instruction and national assessments often focus on CALP, while individual learners may invest more in BICS-related activities. Moreover, teacher quality can vary, and no one assessment perfectly captures learners' proficiency.

Finally, learners shouldn't become overly fixated on the reliability of their self-assessments, not because such an issue lacks importance but rather due to the negative effects of anxiety. The next and final chapter will differentiate between legitimate concern and anxiety, detail the latter's debilitating effects, and recommend ways learners can make this journey less stressful and more enjoyable.

DISCUSSION QUESTIONS

1. Which appeals to you most: a checklist, a questionnaire, or a diary? Explain.
2. Think of a recent speaking performance in the target language. What items on a checklist would you have to assess it? What goals would these items align with?
3. If you were to assess your general competence in a diary, what questions would guide your writing? What goals would these align with?
4. In your current schedule, how frequently could you self-assess? At what times of the day would you engage in it? Explain.
5. What skill (i.e., reading, writing, listening, and speaking) do you feel least prepared to self-assess? Why? How could you address this?

RECOMMENDED READING

MacIntyre, P., Noels, K., & Clément, R. (1997). Biases in self-ratings of second language proficiency: The role of language anxiety. *Language Learning, 47,* 265–287. doi: 10.1111/0023-8333.81997008

This article demonstrates the negative impact anxiety has on self-assessment. The participants—English-speaking learners of French—assessed their performance on several tasks and filled out a questionnaire about language anxiety. The results showed anxiety levels negatively correlated with self-assessment, regardless of learners' abilities indicated on objective assessments.

REFERENCES

ACTFL. (n.d.). NCSSFL-ACTFL can-do statements. Retrieved from https://www.actfl.org/publications/guidelines-and-manuals/ncssfl-actfl-can-do-statements

ACTFL. (2017). Can-do statements. Retrieved from https://www.actfl.org/sites/default/files/CanDos/Novice%20Can-Do_Statements.pdf

Andrade, H., & Du, Y. (2007). Student response to criteria-referenced self-assessment. *Assessment & Evaluation in Higher Education, 32,* 159–181. doi: 10.1080/02602930600801928

Babaii, E., Taghaddomi, S., & Pashmforoosh, R. (2016). Speaking self-assessment: Mismatches between learners' and teachers' criteria. *Language Testing, 33,* 411–437. doi: 10.1177/0265532215590847

Bailey, K. (1991). Diary studies of classroom language learning: The doubting game and the believing game. In E. Sadtono (Ed.), *Language acquisition and the second/foreign language classroom* (pp. 60–102). Singapore: SEAMEO Regional Language Centre.

Brown, D. (2004). *Language assessment: Principles and classroom practices.* Boston: Longman.

Brown, J. (1996). *Testing in language programs.* Upper Saddle River, NJ: Prentice Hall Regents.

Brown, J., & Hudson, T. (1998). The alternatives in language assessment: Advantages and disadvantages. *University of Hawai'i Working Papers in ESL, 16,* 79–103.

Brown, N., Dewey, D., & Cox, T. (2014). Assessing the validity of can-do statements in retrospective (then-now) self-assessment. *Foreign Language Annals, 47,* 261–285. doi: 10.1111/flan.12082

Butler, Y., & Lee, J. (2006). On-task versus off-task self-assessments among Korean elementary school students studying English. *The Modern Language Journal, 90,* 506–517. doi.org/10.1111/j.1540-4781.2006.00463.x

de Saint Léger, D. (2009). Self-assessment of speaking skills and participation in a foreign language class. *Foreign Language Annals, 42,* 158–178. doi: 10.1111/j.1944-9720.2009.01013.x

Diaz-Rico, L. (2008). *Strategies for teaching English learners* (2nd ed.). Boston: Pearson.

Dlaska, A., & Krekeler, C. (2008). Self-assessment of pronunciation. *System, 36,* 506–516. doi:10.1016/j.system.2008.03.003

Flavell, J. (1979). Metacognition and cognitive monitoring. *American Psychologist, 34,* 906–911. doi: 10.1037/0003-066X.34.10.906

Fry, J. (1988). Diary studies in classroom SLA research problems and prospects. *JALT Journal, 9,* 158–167.

Gardner, D. (2000). Self-assessment for autonomous language learners. *Links & Letters, 7,* 49–60.

Huang, S. (2016). Understanding learners' self-assessment and self-feedback on their foreign language speaking performance. *Assessment & Evaluation in Higher Education, 41,* 803–820. doi: 10.1080/02602938.2015.1042426

Kanwit, M., & Geeslin, K. (2014). The interpretation of Spanish subjunctive and indicative forms in adverbial clauses. *Studies in Second Language Acquisition, 36,* 487–533. doi:10.1017/S0272263114000126

Lappin-Fortin, K., & Rye, B. (2014). The use of pre-/posttest and self-assessment tools in a French pronunciation course. *Foreign Language Annals, 47,* 300–320. doi: 10.1111/flan.12083

Leung, C., & Lewkowicz, J. (2006). Expanding horizons and unsolved conundrums: Language testing and assessment. *TESOL Quarterly, 40,* 211–234. doi: 10.2307/40264517

Oxman, A. (1994). Checklists for review articles. *British Medical Journal, 309,* 648–651.

Peirce, B. (1994). Using diaries in second language research and teaching. *English Quarterly, 26,* 22–29.

Porto, M. (2007). Learning diaries in the English as a foreign language classroom: A tool for accessing learners' perceptions of lessons and developing learner autonomy and reflection. *Foreign Language Annals, 40,* 672–696. doi: 10.1111/j.1944- 9720.2007.tb02887.x

Srimavin, W., & Darasawang, P. (2004). Developing self-assessment through journal writing. *Proceedings of the Independent Learning Conference 2003*. Bundoora, Australia.

Suzuki, Y. (2015). Self-assessment of Japanese as a second language: The role of experiences in the naturalistic acquisition. *Language Testing, 32*, 63–81. doi: 10.1177/02655322145418

Trofimovich, P., Isaacs, T., Kennedy, S., Saito, K., & Crowther, D. (2016). Flawed self-assessment: Investigating self- and other-perception of second language speech. *Bilingualism: Language and Cognition, 19*, 122–140. doi:10.1017/S1366728914000832

Truscott, J. (1998). Noticing in second language acquisition: A critical review. *Second Language Research, 14*, 103–135. doi: 10.1191/026765898674803209

Wakita, T., Ueshima, N., & Noguchi, H. (2012). Psychological distance between categories in the Likert scale: Comparing different numbers of options. *Educational and Psychological Measurement, 72*, 533–546. doi: 10.1177/0013164411431162

8

RELAX: IT'S ONLY A LANGUAGE

It would be odd if pursuing another a language didn't generate some unease for monolingual Americans. Learners will devote a significant number of hours to locating interesting and comprehensible materials, engaging them, and assessing personal progress. Travel to foreign countries is probable and much effort will be expended trying to understand the target language's culture (or cultures). Time normally reserved for exercising, reading, and spending time with friends and family may become consumed by language learning. And while this process need not trigger bankruptcy, it will likely represent a significant investment.

Seriously working toward a goal only understood through the experience of others and engaging in an unfamiliar process to achieve it involve many personal firsts and a mix of emotions. The excitement of uttering new phrases coupled with the inevitable feelings of humiliation when grammar errors, pronunciation difficulties, and inaccurate vocabulary present themselves can create self-doubt. Physical reactions such as sweating and an increased heart rate may occur when publicly using the target language—or even thinking about doing so. Stuttering may happen while speaking; searing fear may at times inhibit vocalization altogether.

LANGUAGE LEARNING AND ANXIETY

Anxiety: Definition and Causes

This "apprehension experienced when a situation requires the use of a second language with which the individual is not fully proficient," thereby increasing "the propensity for an individual to react in a nervous manner when speaking, listening, reading, or writing in the second language," is known as *language-learning anxiety* (MacIntyre, as cited in Sheen, 2008, p. 843). *Negative beliefs* (e.g., "I'm not smart enough," "The language is too difficult") are one cause of such anxiety. Research with American university students in beginning-level French, German, Japanese, and Spanish classes found that negative beliefs about academic competence and self-worth predicted high levels of anxiety (Onwuegbuzie, Bailey, & Daley, 1999).

Perfectionism, which results in "excessively high standards for performance accompanied by overly critical self-evaluations" (Gregersen & Horwitz, 2002, p. 563), is a specific type of negative—and erroneous—belief that causes anxiety. A Chilean-based study of university students in second-year English classes highlights the harmfulness of perfectionism. In it, highly anxious learners were compared to peers with low levels of anxiety. The results showed the former were extremely perfectionistic, meaning they held naïve beliefs about what they could and should be able to comprehend and express, which sometimes led to procrastination (Gregersen & Horwitz, 2002).

Gender can also be related to the level of anxiety an individual possesses. Research has found that females generally experience more language-learning anxiety than males. One large-scale study carried out with almost two thousand language learners from ninety nationalities and a variety of education levels compared the anxiety experienced by males and females, in addition to the enjoyment language learning gave them. While females reported significantly more anxiety than males, they also enjoyed language learning significantly more. Such results should be interpreted with caution, as they can't predict the anxiety of individuals, and large numbers of both males and females have low and high levels of anxiety (Dewaele, MacIntyre, Boudreau, & Dewaele, 2016).

Forced speech, or when learners are obligated "to produce language that they have not yet acquired" (Krashen, 2018, p. 1), can cause anxiety.

Being made to speak prior to reaching a certain comfort level with the language promotes tension, frustration, and perhaps even aversion to the language altogether. For decades, Stephen Krashen has steadfastly held the position that such forced speech fails to facilitate linguistic growth (Krashen, 1994, 2014, 2018).

Krashen has detailed the potential harm of anxiety resulting from forced speech in the *affective filter hypothesis*: Learners who experience low levels of anxiety and generally possess positive attitudes toward the learning process absorb more of the comprehensible input to which they are exposed. Moreover, they enthusiastically pursue such input. Conversely, those with high levels of anxiety and negative feelings toward the learning process absorb less comprehensible input and exhibit less enthusiasm when encountering it (Krashen & Terrell, 1998).

Excessive external stimuli combined with performance pressure can create a *tense environment,* which also raises anxiety. A study at the University of Texas separated intermediate-level international students into anxiety and nonanxiety groups. Participants in both groups were interviewed, yet the former encountered a fidgety interviewer and were told the experience measured their English proficiency, while the latter entered a calm environment where they were told to have fun. The results showed participants in the nonanxiety group performed better and had less anxiety (Steinberg & Horwitz, 1986).

Difficulty learning the language is probably the most widely reported cause of anxiety. In a study of Chinese-speaking English learners at various proficiency levels from several Taiwanese universities, difficulty learning English was the strongest predictor of anxiety, responsible for more than one-third of participants' anxiety. The second-largest factor, classroom learning characteristics, explained only 7.3 percent of participants' anxiety (Chen & Chang, 2004).

It is logical to assume that less proficient learners have more anxiety. By extension, more proficient learners should feel less anxiety. Research on undergraduate language learners in China (Liu, 2006) and high school students in the United States (Sparks, Ganschow, Artzer, Siebenhar, & Plageman, 1997) has demonstrated that anxiety levels do, in fact, differ according to proficiency level. However, this relationship between anxiety and proficiency lacks clarity: Is anxiety an integral part of beginning-level language learning that must be overcome, or does anxiety happen to inhibit learning for some more than others (Young, 1986)? Perhaps the unfortunate answer is both are true.

Further complicating the relationship between proficiency and anxiety are findings showing more anxiety among advanced learners. American university students enrolled in first-, second-, and third-year Spanish courses completed a foreign-language-learning anxiety inventory, the results of which revealed significantly higher levels of anxiety among third-year participants. Moreover, those with higher levels of anxiety had better final grades, thereby casting doubt on the notion that increased anxiety always ends in poor performance (Marcos-Llinas & Garau, 2009).

Manifestations of Anxiety

In short, while certain factors may be more likely to cause anxiety, learners of all first languages, genders, and proficiency levels can experience it. Moreover, anxiety can manifest itself in several ways, one of which is *test anxiety*. Of course, this "type of performance anxiety stemming from a fear of failure" (Horwitz, Horwitz, & Cope, 1986, p. 128) isn't limited to language learning: it also occurs in the first language. Physical reactions such as a pounding heart and sweating accompany this added emotional weight, making already challenging assessments overwhelming (Joy, 2013).

Test anxiety negatively and significantly correlated with the oral exam results of intermediate-level learners of French at an American university in one study. In other words, the more anxiety participants possessed, the worse they performed on an assessment which required them to speak about various aspects of culture and participate in various role-plays. Specifically, as anxiety increased, the quantity of words—in addition to the use of dependent clauses and target structures—decreased (Phillips, 1992).

Test anxiety extends beyond the United States and has been observed in many other populations. Within a larger study examining the language-learning enjoyment and anxiety of English learners at various levels at one Chinese university, participants reported that tests triggered intense anxiety, most of which appears to have revolved around listening and speaking. One student noted the insecurity generated by a dictation exam and the frustration experienced following it: "The mid-term listening exam made me feel very nervous because I could not understand the listening material. . . . This made me very disappointed with myself" (Jiang & Dewaele, 2019, p. 20).

Communication apprehension is another manifestation of anxiety. Hesitancy to speak in front of others, whether in small groups or during formal presentations, typifies communication anxiety (Horwitz, Horwitz, & Cope, 1986). Research on Chinese high school–aged students in New Zealand revealed that learners can have several explanations for such apprehension, including the dissimilar motives for speaking in the first language and English, lack of preparation time, and low confidence (Mak & White, 1997).

University students have also exhibited communication apprehension. In one Chinese university, first-year non-English majors enrolled in a required English course completed a number of questionnaires concerned with their disposition to communicate, language-learning anxiety, and proficiency in English. The results showed those who avoided speaking during class possessed negative attitudes toward interpersonal conversations, while the reverse was true for those who spoke frequently in class. Approximately one-third of participants reported feeling anxious, which was significantly related to their unwillingness to talk and proficiency level (Liu & Jackson, 2008).

A third and related manifestation of anxiety is *fear of negative evaluation*. This involves learners feeling scared of how others will view them when using the language. Learners with fear of negative evaluation anticipate looking foolish and suspect their peers and native speakers will harshly judge their ability to use the target language. Such an outlook often leads to refraining from participating in potentially evaluative situations. Unfortunately, this may stop them from speaking in language classes (Horwitz, Horwitz, & Cope, 1986).

The anxiety of social situations also potentially leads to silence and avoidance of socialization. This deprives learners of comprehensible input, practice opportunities, and cultural knowledge. It is not unusual to hear students returning from semester- or year-long study abroad programs speak of a handful of peers who avoided native speakers, socialized exclusively with other Americans, and spent breaks in their room. In addition to time, these students have wasted a tremendous amount of money.

Not surprisingly, research has shown that anxiety has a detrimental impact on learners' willingness to continue studying a language. In a study of American college students enrolled in a variety of languages (e.g., French, German, Japanese, and Spanish) across various proficiency levels, participants who conveyed higher levels of anxiety when comprehending and speaking the target language were more likely to withdraw from their class (Bailey, Onwuegbuzie, & Daley, 2003).

Positive Anxiety?

While most anxiety negatively impacts language learning, there is some evidence for it playing a positive role. Known as *facilitative anxiety*, some anxiety can motivate learners to surmount difficulties (Young, 1994). This was shown in a group of Mexican university students preparing to teach English. Interviews and journals revealed that several had experienced significant personal problems and struggled to do well in classes. However, some noted how the anxiety which accompanied their learning difficulties inspired them to improve (Méndez López & Fabela Cárdenas, 2014).

American university students in their first semester of learning Arabic have also been shown to benefit from anxiety. During an intensive first-year Arabic course, participants completed tasks which required them to read, listen to, and produce language that contained certain grammatical forms. These steps were followed by two tests which sought to measure recognition and production of such forms, the results of which showed that higher anxiety positively correlated with both. One explanation is that higher levels of anxiety could represent a type of linguistic hypervigilance and sensitivity to input (Nassif, 2019).

While these studies demonstrate the potentially facilitative role for anxiety, they should be viewed with caution, principally because they represent outliers. Most studies point to the debilitating or negative influence of anxiety on language learning. Moreover, constant anxiety is severely unpleasant; encouraging it constitutes unnecessary cruelty. Fortunately, learners can help reduce the amount of anxiety they possess and make language learning an agreeable experience, if not one that brings great satisfaction.

GOD HELPS THOSE WHO HELP THEMSELVES

Becoming Aware

The first step learners can take is to recognize their anxiety. Even though learners often feel anxiety and can express these feelings to themselves and others, they can't identify the factors which cause them. Without this insight, approaches to reducing anxiety may lack effectiveness. Developing such awareness can occur by completing an anxiety questionnaire, one of which is the *Foreign Language Classroom Anxiety Scale* (FLCAS). Several items on the instrument relate to test anxiety (e.g., "The more I study for a language test, the more confused I get," and "I am usually at ease during tests in my language class") (Horwitz, Horwitz, & Cope, 1986, p. 129).

Other items pertain to *communication apprehension*, such as "I get nervous and confused when I am speaking in my language class," and "In language class, I can get so nervous I forget things I know." The last category of items concerns *negative evaluation* (e.g., "I am afraid that the other students will laugh at me when I speak," and "I am afraid that my language teacher is ready to correct every mistake I make") (Horwitz, Horwitz, & Cope, 1986, p. 129–130). The instrument is scored on a 5-point Likert scale, ranging from 1 (strongly agree) to 5 (strongly disagree) and contains thirty items, enabling learners to fill it out in a reasonable amount of time.

While survey instruments can bring awareness, learners should also note their physical and emotional reactions during language use. In addition to a pounding heart, increased perspiration, headaches, muscle pain, nail biting, hair twirling, and playing with objects such as pens and pencils can occur. Learners can experience uncharacteristic memory lapses, stutter, and seem skittish. Some may refrain from making eye contact with interlocutors, exhibit distorted facial expressions, and make negative statements about themselves (e.g., "My Spanish sucks!") (Oxford, 1999).

Noting them can shed light on anxiety-provoking aspects of language learning which they may not recall when completing a questionnaire or which the instrument may not address. Certain forms of oral correction, for instance, have been shown to incite more anxiety than others. Advanced English language learners from a variety of first languages in one American university reported that open-ended questions which consisted simply of "What?" raised anxiety levels, presumably because they couldn't determine the error. Conversely, "recognizing their errors and knowing how to fix them" decreased their anxiety (Lee, 2016, p. 86).

Learners could jot down this and similar information in a diary or on a notecard following particularly uncomfortable interactions. For example: A highly proficient speaker of Arabic might feel distressed upon meeting native speakers of the language. His heart beats quickly when they initiate questions about how he learned Arabic and use unfamiliar terms. Following these occurrences, he records words like *native speakers*, *questions*, *vocabulary*. Later examination of his notes reveals not only that open-ended questions not only trigger his anxiety but also that his Arabic is highly formal and that he lacks understanding of localized varieties of the language limited to the spoken realm.

Possessing Realistic Beliefs

The learner then takes the obvious step of trying to expand his knowledge of Arabic. However, he should also adopt realistic beliefs about his depth of knowledge. As discussed above, perfectionistic individuals make incorrect assumptions about the nature of language learning and their abilities. Expecting to understand everything which emerges from a native speaker's mouth—especially when it conveys highly particular linguistic patterns—is also erroneous, and "when beliefs and reality clash, anxiety results" (Young, 1991, p. 428). Learning will never end, and trying to become a database of the entire Arabic language is futile.

The most anxiety-provoking belief probably regards accent; as discussed in chapter 2, adult learners will likely never acquire a native-like accent. Moreover, certain grammatical forms (e.g., prepositions) will doubtfully ever be uttered with 100 percent accuracy. Because native speakers often erroneously judge non-native speakers' proficiency on the basis of these two elements, they receive much attention and therefore needle learners' sense of self-worth.

The application of rational emotive therapy can help learners identify irrational beliefs which trigger anxiety, enabling them to "interpret such situations in more realistic ways" (Foss & Reitzel, 1988, p. 445). To do so, learners should ask themselves the three following questions: (1) What irrational belief do I want to dispute? (2) What evidence exists of the falseness of this belief? and (3) Does evidence exist of the truthfulness of this belief? (p. 446). Answers should demonstrate the erroneousness of their beliefs and thereby diminish anxiety.

Ignoring Ignorance and Avoiding Harmful People

Flawed beliefs about language learning are ubiquitous in popular culture. Not all warrant confrontation; some can simply be ignored. Unfortunately, when humans repeatedly hear a specific claim—whether in their own head or from others—they tend to accept it as true, even when no available evidence supports it or mountains of evidence cast severe doubt on it (DiFonzo, 2011; Schwarz, Sanna, Skurnik, & Yoon, 2007). Therefore, learners should periodically remind themselves of the meritless nature of these beliefs, lest they consciously or subconsciously risk adopting them.

Avoiding individuals who promote them or otherwise trigger anxiety is also advisable. When economic factors prevent escaping harmful people, or completing a program necessitates taking classes with a teacher who exacerbates a learner's anxiety, this advice may lack practicality. Nevertheless, negative surroundings can decrease motivation and encourage burnout (Leiter & Maslach, 1988); getting away from them is necessary for continued growth and overall emotional wellness. Socializing with new individuals and switching instructors might bring temporary awkwardness, but the benefits will eventually become evident.

Accepting the Sounds of Silence

Learners can take other steps to avoid engaging in actions they know will cause them to feel more anxious, one of which is forced speech. As discussed above, Krashen (1994, 2014, 2018) has outlined how instructors harm learners when they prematurely obligate them to produce oral language. However, learners also can expect unrealistic and unnecessary amounts of output. Instead of subjecting themselves to the constant stress of formulating utterances, learners can relax and focus on obtaining comprehensible input that will later naturally transform into output.

Engaging in Positive Self-Talk

The avoidance of negative people and practices may rescue learners from harm, but it doesn't help them escape spontaneous instances of anxiety. For this to occur, positive self-talk is necessary (Tasnimi, 2009; Woodrow, 2006). While the same pronouncements won't work for everybody, generic statements which affirm the ability to carry out a language task, (e.g., "Come on, you got this") provide reassurance about learners' abilities (e.g., "If billions of other people can do this, so can I") and encourage calm (e.g., "Relax—you're going to go in there and speak; it is no big deal") offer starting points from which to customize positive self-talk.

Positive self-talk was the most commonly used strategy in a study of first- and second-year non-English majors at a Chinese university. Anxious learners helped themselves by noting they were just as capable as their peers; anxiety would cease or diminish through concrete behaviors; language learning requires patience and tenacity; energy devoted toward language learning is the most significant factor in determining success; and feelings of anxiety are normal (Guo, Xu, & Liu, 2018).

Even among experienced learners, possessing a positive orientation is vital for maintaining manageable levels of anxiety, and learners with it "tend to be open to pleasant moments, to be more sensitive to signals of reward from teachers or peers, and to view setbacks in learning as less threatening" (Jin & Dewaele, 2018, p. 154). A study of English majors at another Chinese university showed orientation to be the most significant factor associated with anxiety levels. Participants with higher levels of anxiety were inclined to have a negative orientation, while those with lower levels of anxiety projected more positivity toward themselves and the learning process (Jin & Dewaele, 2018).

Laughing about It

Research has shown that laughter is important for good overall health (Mora-Ripoll, 2010), improves general learning (Savage, Lujan, Thipparthi, & DiCarlo, 2017), and can reduce anxiety during formal language instruction (Wagner & Urios-Aparisi, 2011). Language learners must laugh at themselves and the target language to reduce stress and normalize their feelings. Otherwise, they risk viewing the process with an unpleasant degree of seriousness and any comments on their use of the target language as direct attacks on their self-worth. Besides, the miscommunication resulting from learner errors often involves great silliness.

The world of humor offers insight into how language learners make light of their limitations. British comedian Eddie Izzard performs live shows in English, Spanish, German, and French. He realizes that he makes grammar errors, mispronounces words, and incorrectly uses vocabulary, but he doesn't mind; he aims to communicate. In fact, part of his act involves verbatim English translations into French. Goofy utterances and scenarios that all language learners can relate to often emerge (FRANCE 24 English, 2018).

South African entertainer Trevor Noah grew up speaking multiple languages, yet only started studying his father's native German in adulthood. When he visited Germany, he felt perplexed by the pained facial expressions which greeted his words. After this occurred a few times, he asked a friend what was going on, and she reluctantly responded that his tone and intonation made him sound like Hitler (*The Daily Show with Trevor Noah*, 2019)! Although many may find humor that invokes Adolf Hitler distasteful and offensive, most learners can relate to the vocal changes which occur when speaking another language. On more than one occasion, the author has been told he sounds like a Colombian woman (i.e., his wife).

Moroccan-born comedian Gad Elmaleh was already an established comedian when he decided to learn English and restart his career in the United States. Not only does he note that the humor of certain American expressions is nonexistent in the other languages he speaks—Arabic and French (e.g., browsing)—but like Trevor Noah, he discusses the frustration which accompanies stressing the wrong syllable on a word: "One day, I said to a friend of mine. He's American. I went on VEYcation. He said, 'What's that?' And then he said 'You mean a vaCAYtion.' And they don't meet me halfway. That's a problem" (Team Coco, 2018, 44).

Although he isn't a comedian, best-selling author David Sedaris's nonfiction frequently dives into his personal struggles, learning French among them. The number of anxiety-provoking situations he faced when he moved to Paris seems almost unbearable—all of them funny, however. In his first French class, he felt inferior to his classmates, who possessed a "confidence I found intimidating. As an added discomfort, they were all young, attractive, and well dressed, causing me to feel not unlike Pa Kettle trapped backstage after a fashion show" (Sedaris, 2007, para. 1).

Aside from sheer laughter, learners can take away something very important from these entertainers: in spite of their talent and fame, they experience the same struggles as other language learners. They remind peers of the challenges inherent in the language-learning process and suggest they approach them with a degree of levity. Thus, if an American male tells his Colombian sister-in-law that he likes her body (*cuerpo*) when he means her portrait (*cuadro*), the world won't end. Likewise, if he tells his Spanish cousin that his father and her father have the same breasts (*senos*) instead of eyebrows (*cejas*), self-flagellation isn't in order.

Solidarity

Knowing that others have similar experiences and share the same emotions produces a sense of solidarity and reminds learners they aren't alone. Isolation damages mental health and can lead humans to second-guess life decisions (Cacioppo & Hawkley, 2003). In the United States, language learners are especially susceptible to such feelings because of the small number of peers who share similar goals. Research has also found that lack of peer contact damages motivation. Rachel, a college student in a self-directed Russian program, felt it was difficult "to remember why I'm [studying Russian] if no one else is doing it. I feel kind of like I'm learning in a box" (Bown, 2006, p. 649).

Research likewise has highlighted the connection between anxiety and peer support. Learners of French, German, and Spanish in American community colleges reported that friendship and a feeling of community diminished their anxiety (Samimy & Rardin, 1994; von Wörde, 2003). If learners aren't participating in a language class, they can meet like-minded individuals in language exchange groups which facilitate informal conversations in a variety of settings, including university campuses, community centers, bars, and even online.

These interactions give learners the opportunity to express their frustrations with people who share similar feelings and gain insight into how to overcome difficulties. Meeting advanced learners from a similar background also normalizes the process of language learning and can restore belief in one's ability to succeed. However, learners should show restraint when voicing negative feelings and discussing anxiety, not because they lack importance but rather because they can become all-consuming and lead learners to ignore opportunities for growth and enjoyment.

Listen to the Music

Research has long documented the cognitive value of playing background music in both the first and foreign languages (de Groot, 2006). Learners can also temporarily decrease their anxiety levels by listening to music (Oxford & Shearin, 1994). For example, to ease nerves before giving a speech or meeting native speakers at a party, they can turn on calming music, take a walk, and focus on their breathing. After an intense experience—negative or positive—learners can cool down using the same procedure.

RELAX: NOBODY DIES

Whether learners use music or any of the other recommendations to decrease anxiety, they should not expect the same action to work in all settings. Like all aspects of language learning, anxiety is dynamic and can change depending on task and environment. Anxiety may manifest itself differently as learners grow, and effectively reducing it might require dissimilar approaches at the beginning, intermediate, and advanced levels. Such information alone could induce panic, but it is simply reality.

A FINAL THOUGHT

Besides, learners should have faith in themselves. They have the faculties to learn, just like billions of other human beings. It will take time, and it will involve frustration, but tenacity and thoughtfulness will lead to wonderful outcomes. Along the way, setbacks will occur, as will embarrassing moments, but most have nothing to do with negative intentions, lack of ability, or poor effort. They're just natural. No fortunes are lost, no long-term environmental disasters come about, and nobody dies because of language-learning anxiety. Learners should take comfort knowing that others have experienced identical insecurities.

DISCUSSION QUESTIONS

1. What sort of anxiety do you have: test anxiety, communication apprehension, and/or fear of negative evaluation?
2. What do you think the causes of your anxiety are?
3. How are you aware of your anxiety? After reading this chapter, what do you think you will change about monitoring your anxiety?
4. Before you read this chapter, how did you cope with anxiety?
5. Now that you have read this chapter, what new steps will you take to decrease your anxiety?

RECOMMENDED READING

Cohen, A. (2001). From L1 to L2: The confessions of a sometimes frustrated multiliterate. In D. Belcher & U. Connor (Eds.), *Reflections on multiliterate lives* (pp. 79–95). Clevedon, UK: Multilingual Matters.

In this chapter, a renowned linguist and retired professor at the University of Minnesota describes his experiences studying a dozen languages. Although Andrew Cohen has expertise in language learning, he demonstrates he is not immune to the frustration felt by nonspecialists. Of particular interest is his relationship with Hebrew, a language to which he was introduced in childhood and studied during his sixteen years of living in Israel.

REFERENCES

Bailey, P., Onwuegbuzie, A., & Daley, C. (2003). Foreign language anxiety and student attrition. *Academic Exchange Quarterly, 7,* 304–308.

Bown, J. (2006). Locus on learning and affective strategy use: Two factors affecting success in self-instructed language learning. *Foreign Language Annals, 39,* 640–659. doi: 10.1111/j.1944-9720.2006.tb02281.x

Cacioppo, J., & Hawkley, L. (2003). Social isolation and health, with an emphasis on underlying mechanisms. *Perspectives in Biology and Medicine, 46,* S39–S52. doi: 10.1353/pbm.2003.0063

Chen, T., & Chang, G. (2004). The relationship between foreign language anxiety and learning difficulties. *Foreign Language Annals, 37,* 279–289. doi: 10.1111/j.1944-9720.2004.tb02200.x de Groot, A. (2006). Effects of stimulus characteristics and background music on foreign language vocabulary learning and forgetting. *Language Learning, 56*, 463–506. doi: 10.1111/j.1467-9922.2006.00374.x

Dewaele, J., MacIntyre, P., Boudreau, C., & Dewaele, L. (2016). Do girls have all the fun? Anxiety and enjoyment in the foreign language classroom. *Theory and Practice of Second Language Acquisition, 2*, 41–63.

DiFonzo, N. (2011, April 22). The echo-chamber effect. *The New York Times*. Retrieved from https://www.nytimes.com/roomfordebate/2011/04/21/barack-obama-and-the-psychology-of-the-birther-myth/the-echo-chamber-effect

Foss, K., & Reitzel, A. (1988). A relational model for managing second language anxiety. *TESOL Quarterly, 22*, 437–454. doi: 10.2307/3587288

FRANCE 24 English (2018, January 12). *Eddie Izzard on French grammar, Brexit and trying to get his mother back* [Video file]. Retrieved from https://www.youtube.com/watch?v=xVageBoD7v4

Gregersen, T., & Horwitz, E. (2002). Language learning and perfectionism: Anxious and non-anxious language learners' reactions to their own oral performance. *The Modern Language Journal, 86*, 562–570. doi: 10.1111/1540-4781.00161

Guo, Y., Xu, J., & Liu, X. (2018). English language learners' use of self-regulatory strategies for foreign language anxiety in China. *System, 76*, 49–61. doi: 10.1016/j.system.2018.05.001

Horwitz, E., Horwitz, M., & Cope, J. (1986). Foreign language classroom anxiety. *The Modern Language Journal, 70*, 125–132. doi: 10.1111/j.1540-4781.1986.tb05256.x

Jiang, Y., & Dewaele, J. (2019). How unique is the foreign language classroom enjoyment and anxiety of Chinese EFL learners? *System, 19*, 13–25. doi: 10.1016/j.system.2019.02.017

Jin, Y., & Dewaele, J. (2018). The effect of positive orientation and perceived social support on foreign language classroom anxiety. *System, 74*, 149–157. doi: 10.1016/j.system.2018.01.002

Joy, J. (2013). The altitude of test anxiety among second language learners. *Language Testing in Asia, 3*, 1–8. doi: 10.1186/2229-0443-3-10

Krashen, S. (1994). The pleasure hypothesis. In J. Alatis (Ed.), *Georgetown University round-table of languages and linguistics* (pp. 299–322). Washington, D.C.: Georgetown University Press.

Krashen, S. (2014). The comprehension hypothesis and animal language. In J. Horváth & P. Medgyes (Eds.), *Studies in honour of Marianne Nikolov* (pp. 243–258). Pécs, Hungary: Lingua Franca Csoport.

Krashen, S. (2018). Down with forced speech. Retrieved from http://www.sdkrashen.com/content/articles/down_with_forced_speech_pdf.pdf

Krashen, S., & Terrell, T. (1998). *The natural approach: Language acquisition in the class-room.* New York: Prentice-Hall.

Lee, E. (2016). Reducing international graduate students' language anxiety through oral pronunciation corrections. *System, 56*, 78–95. doi: 10.1016/j.system.2015.11.006

Leiter, M., & Maslach, C. (1988). The impact of interpersonal environment on burnout and organizational commitment. *Journal of Organizational Behavior, 9*, 297–308. doi: 10.1002/job.4030090402

Liu, M. (2006). Anxiety in Chinese EFL students at different proficiency levels. *System, 34*, 301–316. doi:10.1016/j.system.2006.04.004

Liu, M., & Jackson, J. (2008). An exploration of Chinese EFL learners' unwillingness to communicate and foreign language anxiety. *The Modern Language Journal, 92*, 71–86. doi: 10.1111/j.1540-4781.2008.00687.x

Mak, B., & White, C. (1997). Communication apprehension of Chinese ESL students. *Hong Kong Journal of Applied Linguistics, 2*, 81–95.

Marcos-Llinas, M., & Garau, M. (2009). Effects of language anxiety on three proficiency-level courses of Spanish as a foreign language. *Foreign Language Annals, 42*, 94–111. doi: 10.1111/j.1944-9720.2004.tb02200.x

Méndez López, M., & Fabela Cárdenas, M. (2014). Emotions and their effects in a language learning Mexican context. *System, 42*, 298–307. doi:10.1016/j.system.2013.12.006

Mora-Ripoll, R. (2010). The therapeutic value of laughter in medicine. *Alternative Therapies, 16,* 56–64.

Nassif, L. (2019). The relationship of language anxiety with noticing and oral production of L2 forms: A study of beginning learners of Arabic. *System, 80,* 304–317. doi: 10.1016/j.system.2018.12.008

Onwuegbuzie, A., Bailey, P., & Daley, C. (1999). Factors associated with foreign language anxiety. *Applied Psycholinguistics, 20,* 217–239. doi: 10.1017/S0142716499002039

Oxford, R. (1999). Anxiety and the language learner: New insights. In J. Arnold (Ed.), *Affect in language learning* (pp. 58–67). New York: Cambridge University Press.

Oxford, R., & Shearin, J. (1994). Language learning motivation: Expanding the theoretical framework. *The Modern Language Journal, 78,* 12–28. doi: 10.1111/j.1540-4781.1994.tb02011.x

Phillips, E. (1992). The effects of language anxiety on students' oral test performance and attitudes. *The Modern Language Journal, 76,* 14–26. doi: 10.2307/329894

Samimy, K., & Rardin, J. (1994). Adult language learners' affective reactions to community language learning: A descriptive study. *Foreign Language Annals, 27,* 379–390. doi:10.1111/j.1944-9720.1994.tb01215.x

Savage, B., Lujan, H., Thipparthi, R., & DiCarlo, S. (2017). Humor, laughter, learning, and health! A brief review. *Advances in Physiology Education, 41,* 341–347. doi: 10.1152/advan.00030.2017

Schwarz, N., Sanna, L., Skurnik, I., & Yoon, C. (2007). Metacognitive experiences and the intricacies of setting people straight: Implications for debiasing and public information campaigns. *Advances in Experimental Social Psychology, 39,* 127–161. doi: 10.1016/S0065-2601(06)39003-X

Sedaris, D. (2007, January 20). Me talk pretty one day. *Esquire.* Retrieved from https://www.esquire.com/lifestyle/a1419/talk-pretty-0399/

Sheen, Y. (2008). Recasts, language anxiety, modified output, and L2 learning. *Language Learning, 58,* 835–874. doi: 10.1111/j.1467-9922.2008.00480.x

Sparks, R., Ganschow, L., Artzer, M., Siebenhar, D., & Plageman, M. (1997). Language anxiety and proficiency in a foreign language. *Perceptual and Motor Skills, 85,* 559–562. doi: 10.2466/pms.1997.85.2.559

Steinberg, F., & Horwitz, E. (1986). The effect of induced anxiety on the denotative and interpretive content of second language speech. *TESOL Quarterly, 20,* 131–136. doi: 10.2307/3586395

Tasnimi, M. (2009). Affective factors: Anxiety. *Pan-Pacific Association of Applied Linguistics, 13,* 117–124.

Team Coco (2018, March 2). *Gad Elmaleh points out the absurdities in the English language—CONAN on TBS* [Video file]. Retrieved from https://www.youtube.com/watch?v=1syXYTG4qVY

The Daily Show with Trevor Noah (2019, April 1). When learning German goes wrong—between the scenes [Video file]. Retrieved from https://www.youtube.com/watch?v=79HsZG5piGg

von Wörde, R. (2003). Students' perspectives on foreign language anxiety. *Inquiry, 8*(1), 1–15.

Wagner, M., & Urios-Aparisi, E. (2011). The use of humor in the foreign language classroom: Funny and effective? *Humor, 24,* 399–434. doi: 10.1515/HUMR.2011.024

Woodrow, L. (2006). Anxiety and speaking English as a second language. *Regional Language Centre Journal, 37,* 308–328. doi: 10.1177/0033688206071315

Young, D. (1986). The relationship between anxiety and foreign language oral proficiency ratings. *Foreign Language Annals, 19,* 439–445. doi:10.1111/j.1944-9720.1986.tb01032.x

Young, D. (1991). Creating a low-anxiety classroom environment: What does language anxiety research suggest? *The Modern Language Journal, 75,* 426–439. doi:10.1111/j.1540-4781.1991.tb05378.x

Young, D. (1994). New directions in language anxiety research. In C. Klee (Ed.), *Faces in a crowd: The individual in multisection courses* (pp. 3–46). Boston: Heinle & Heinle.

ABOUT THE AUTHOR

Alex Poole, PhD, is an applied linguist and professor of English at Western Kentucky University. His research interests include Spanish-English bilingualism, grammar instruction, and reading strategies. He regularly publishes his work in academic journals and presents at national and international conferences. He teaches courses on language acquisition, the history of English, language pedagogy, grammar, and composition.